POEMS
THAT MAKE
GROWN
WOMEN CRY

POEMS THAT MAKE GROWN WOMEN CRY

Edited by

ANTHONY and BEN HOLDEN

SIMON & SCHUSTER

NEW YORK   LONDON   TORONTO   SYDNEY   NEW DELHI

Simon & Schuster
1230 Avenue of the Americas
New York, NY 10020

This book is a work of fiction. Any references to historical events,
real people, or real places are used fictitiously. Other names, characters,
places, and events are products of the author's imagination, and any
resemblance to actual events or places or persons, living
or dead, is entirely coincidental.

Copyright © 2016 by Anthony and Ben Holden
Originally published in Great Britain in 2016 by Simon & Schuster UK Ltd.

All rights reserved, including the right to reproduce this
book or portions thereof in any form whatsoever.
For information address Simon & Schuster Subsidiary Rights
Department, 1230 Avenue of the Americas, New York, NY 10020

First Simon & Schuster hardcover edition May 2016

SIMON & SCHUSTER and colophon are registered trademarks of Simon & Schuster, Inc.

For information about special discounts for bulk purchases,
please contact Simon & Schuster Special Sales at 1-866-506-1949 or
business@simonandschuster.com

The Simon & Schuster Speakers Bureau can
bring authors to your live event. For more information or
to book an event contact the Simon & Schuster Speakers
Bureau at 1-866-248-3049 or visit our website at
www.simonspeakers.com.

Interior design by M Rules
Jacket design by Jason Heuer

Manufactured in the UK

1 3 5 7 9 10 8 6 4 2

Library of Congress Cataloging-in-Publication Data

ISBN 978-1-5011-2185-2
ISBN 978-1-5011-2187-6 (ebook)

Contents

Preface

ANTHONY HOLDEN

Yes, I hear you thinking, it makes perfect sense that a father-and-son team should co-edit a book by women about women for ... no, not just women, but *anyone* to read – anyone, that is, interested in the human condition as uniquely observed and distilled by poetry.

Ben and I started planning *Poems That Make Grown Women Cry* while we were still working on its masculine predecessor. At that stage we had no idea how *Poems That Make Grown Men Cry* would fare; perhaps no publisher would be interested in a sister volume? When the male anthology received a startling amount of publicity, even basking awhile in the bestseller lists, we knew we could proceed as planned.

The male title was, of course, deliberately provocative, but also leavened (or so we liked to think) by a hint of self-satire. Clearly, it challenged the hoary stereotype that grown men don't cry – or aren't supposed to, anyway, whether in private or in public. And it seemed to succeed. Its built-in argument was that men should these days be much more in touch with their emotions than in the bygone, stiff-upper-lip days of Empire, and content to display them openly. So we were delighted when this proved the main topic of discussion in countless media and book festival interviews, apparently finding approving echoes around the nation.

But we knew that the male anthology would seem incomplete without a female counterpart, or companion volume. And now, as Ben's background in film moved him to point out, we had the makings of a brand. For all my alternative suggestions, the title had to repeat the same formula. I was more concerned about the currency of the phrase 'grown women' than the dim, uncomprehending charges of sexism that had in some quarters greeted the first book – reeking, to me, of an all too familiar sense-of-humour failure.

When it came to making approaches, however, the old stereotypes were again turned on their heads. Many more women than men told me they didn't weep at anything; I received more polite refusals from eminent women than I had from their male counterparts.

But the vast majority who did respond have again made a wonderful variety of choices, which they explain with potent, often moving resonance. Individually, they strike notes sometimes interestingly similar to the men's, sometimes intriguingly different. Collectively, they again meet my definition of the aspiration of both anthologies: to introduce new readers to the wonders of poetry while surprising the cognoscenti with less familiar marvels.

This collection contains almost 100 poems from eighteen countries, chosen by women of twenty-three nationalities, ranging in age from their twenties to their late nineties. Whereas 75 per cent of the men chose twentieth-century poems – perhaps inevitable, as I mused at the time, so early in the next – only slightly more than 50 per cent of our women have done the same. One-fifth of their choices pre-date the twentieth century; all of a quarter are twenty-first century. The most recent choice was written as we were compiling the book, while the Somali poet Warsan Shire's 2009 poem 'Home' kept striking an especially poignant note during Europe's long, agonizing refugee crisis.

It is no surprise that, whereas the men chose only twelve poems by female poets, the women have picked twice as many. Top of the lachrymose charts this time around comes Emily Dickinson, with three entries, alongside W. B. Yeats, astonishingly missing from the male nominees; joining Elizabeth Bishop in second place with two entries each are Seamus Heaney and W. H. Auden, as well as two other poets neglected by the male contributors, Tennyson and T. S. Eliot.

Alongside Auden, Philip Larkin was the male favourite, with five entries each; in this female volume, he merits only one. The other two masculine favourites, Thomas Hardy and A. E. Housman, are this time strikingly conspicuous by their absence. Ted Hughes and Sylvia Plath, neither of whom figured in the male version, are picked once each. Pablo Neruda earns one male nod, two female.

Meanwhile, there are some interesting overlaps between the two collections. Two playwrights (Tena Štivičić and David Edgar) have both chosen extracts from Shelley's rousing epic *The Masque of Anarchy*. Two novelists (Siri Hustvedt and Douglas Kennedy) have chosen the same profound Emily Dickinson poem, 'After great pain'. John Clare's desolate 'I Am' is the choice of Helen Pankhurst, as it was of Ken Loach; Edward Thomas's nostalgic 'Adlestrop' that of Kate Atkinson and Lynn Barber as well as Simon Winchester. Coleridge's 'Frost at Midnight' is nominated by Helen Macdonald, as it was by Sebastian Faulks.

The Olympic athlete Emma Pooley has gone for the same Wilfred Owen poem, 'Anthem for Doomed Youth', which moved John Humphrys to tears when we discussed the first book on BBC Radio 4's *Today* programme. The broadcaster Mariella Frostrup has chosen the same Yeats poem which had Jeremy Vine choking up while reciting it from memory on his Radio 2 show.

Where Salman Rushdie was profoundly moved by Auden's elegy for Yeats, so is Shami Chakrabarti by his elegy for Freud. Ezra Pound is the choice of the classicist Mary Beard, as he was of the poet Craig Raine, John Updike of Tina Brown and Joseph O'Neill; Harold Pinter the choice of his widow, Antonia Fraser, as he was of Neil LaBute; Gwendolyn Brooks of the American poets Nikki Giovanni and Terrance Hayes; Adrienne Rich of Kate Mosse and Anish Kapoor; Derek Walcott of Chimamanda Ngozi Adichie as well as Mark Haddon and Tom Hiddleston. Shakespeare is the poet for Marina Warner, as for Melvyn Bragg. One of Douglas Dunn's cycle of touching poems in memory of his wife, *Elegies*, is the choice of Juliet Stevenson, as was another of Richard Eyre.

This book also features the same pleasing 'circularity' as its predecessor, with a poem by one of our contributors, the poet laureate Carol Ann Duffy, the choice of another, Imtiaz Dharker, one of whose own has been singled out by Meera Syal.

As in the male book, several pairs of contributors happen to have named the same poem, some of whose writers were also among the male nominees. Seamus Heaney's sonnet cycle 'Clearances', for instance, has been chosen by both Zoë Heller and Sarah Waters; in the male book, Heaney was cited by Richard Curtis and Terry George (while himself opting for Thomas Hardy).

W. B. Yeats's 'The Song of Wandering Aengus' is the choice of Joanne Harris and Carol Ann Duffy; Byron's 'So, we'll go no more a roving' that of Judi Dench and Emily Mortimer; Anna Akhmatova's *Requiem* that of the writer Anne Applebaum and Kate Allen, Director of Amnesty International UK.

The poets of the First World War again feature prominently, with Wilfred Owen chosen by Vanessa Redgrave as he was by Christopher Hitchens, Siegfried Sassoon by Annie Lennox and Allie Esiri as by Barry Humphries. A less well-known WWI poem, this time written by a woman, has been offered a wider audience by Maxine Peake.

Are the women's choices more political? I will leave such delicate issues to Sebastian Faulks, who has the last word in this female anthology as did the late Nadine Gordimer in the male. Suffice it to say here that, thanks to our inspirational partnership with Amnesty International, we again have many contributors with harrowing tales to tell, who have since turned their suffering to the world's advantage by campaigning tirelessly for human rights.

This collection brims with empathy, with fellow-feeling – for human beings, of course, but also for animals, birds, even oysters. There are touching examinations of parent-child relationships, haunting explorations of depression, mental illness, AIDS, adoption, miscarriage. Amid nostalgia for a better past, and protest at the brutish present – we are still living in a world, as Amnesty's Nicky Parker points out in her essay, where women have been put to death for writing poems – there are searing accounts of prejudice, racial or otherwise, of failures to communicate, of persecution and the plight of refugees, alongside passionate pleas for freedom.

As with the male book, other themes range from mortality via pity, pain and loss to the beauty and variety of nature, as well as love in all its many guises – collectively, for me, adding up to a quintessentially poetic sense of yearning, often for missed opportunities. Some choices are almost unbearably intimate: Antonia Fraser and Yoko Ono have both chosen the last poem their eminent husbands wrote for them before their deaths. Claire Tomalin has proudly made public a heart-rending poem by her twenty-two-year-old daughter prefiguring her own death months later.

It is naturally our hope that you will be moved by these remarkable poems, as indeed by the reasons for choosing them offered by our diverse range of distinguished contributors. Why do we want to inflict upon you so delicious a blend of pleasure and pain? Again, as last time around, I will leave Ben to explain.

BEN HOLDEN

For me, this all started with a title.

The reason I phoned my dad in December 2011, twenty-some years since a conversation he'd been having with friends, was that title. He and I should really have a go at making a book out of it. *Poems That Make Grown Men Cry.*

My day job is in feature films, an industry that frequently requires reductive thinking, as complex concepts are encapsulated pithily, from pitch through to poster. This title fitted that bill. It immediately grabbed attention, succinctly heralding a big idea. It was self-explanatory and blunt-edged; yet provoked a variety of conversations. Simple yet far from simplistic.

Crying and poetry are, in their different ways, articulations of the inexpressible (as Pope famously said, poetry exquisitely captures 'what oft was thought, but ne'er so well expressed'). They are, with music, and ironically in the case of poetry, the means by which we humans can explain what we are feeling *when words fail us*. They cut to the quick of our basic condition.

This project would not only allow us to explore this symmetry but also – we hoped – prompt people to read poetry. We wanted to provoke, with the help of distinguished and inspirational contributors, some complex conversations: about our partners Amnesty International and freedom of expression, literacy, emotion and – of course – gender identity. There was also an incontrovertible truth underpinning the title, one that presently causes me slight disquiet.

I am the father of seven-year-old boy-girl twins. Since birth, they have cried with equal facility. Yet statistically, at the age of around ten, my son's tears will most likely dry up. He will stop crying, despite the male tear duct being bigger than the female. I attribute this to cultural conditioning as much as biology. Considering that a sob is a cleansing release as natural as a laugh – sluicing the bloodstream of a hormonal imbalance caused by overwhelming emotion or stress – this sorry fact is a crying shame.

Although perhaps there is hope for my boy yet. As I grow older, my emotional axis having shifted since their births, I find myself crying (or, at least, choking up) a little more. Those stubborn ducts are loosening. This was proven during the launch of our anthology. My ever-lachrymose dad and I were continually moved upon its publication, two-and-a-half years after that wintry phone call. The most rewarding responses were not so much from reviewers as from readers who told us directly that they had found solace and hope in the book's pages: the grieving new widower, the mourning mother, the bereft son. Apparently within the collection – and now this book as well – reside, in Wordsworth's words, 'thoughts that do often lie too deep [even] for tears'.

It was unsurprising, of course, that some commentators found that title gimmicky (*Good, it's working*, I thought). I was not anticipating, however, the vitriol that swung our book's way from a handful of female commentators who seemed intent on missing the point. The most acerbic response came from a BBC Radio 4 presenter who, upon hearing the title for the first time – uttered live on her programme by its guest Professor John Carey – declared that she would like to 'hurl that book across the room'.

At the back of her missile, the broadcaster would have discovered two Afterwords. Women, rightly, had the last word. I would like to borrow from those pieces at the outset of this new collection.

The late, great Nadine Gordimer wrote:

Pablo Neruda's line: 'Whoever discovers who I am will discover who you are.' I am not a man, neither will be the many women who read and receive the revelations of these poems. But in the lives of the great Neruda and other poets harvested here – whoever you are, man, woman or any other gender – you will discover in yourself matchlessly conveyed the exultation and devastation of human experience . . .

Kate Allen, Amnesty International's UK Director and a contributor to this new collection, then observed:

> This anthology might be accused of sexism because it deliberately excludes women contributors. Others may mock the very idea of men crying over poetry. But this is another reason why we at Amnesty are interested in it. It directly addresses the assumption bordering on cliché that women are more emotional – weaker – than men . . . We know that bottling up emotions can lead to aggression. More than this, gender stereotyping is dangerous because it represses ability and ambition, it encourages discrimination and it upholds social inequalities that are a root cause of violence.

We had always intended a twin-sister anthology. We are so proud that she is now here – but, once again, please be clear, this new collection is no less for men than women. Our brilliant 100 female contributors and their poetic selections, just as with the grown men's, speak to us all. Indeed I challenge all blokes out there to read this book with pride – on their daily commute, for example.

How pathetic that this proposition – a man publicly reading a book called *Poems That Make Grown Women Cry* – should still feel somehow daring. Any gender-based conversation in 2016 involves everyone, men and women. Feminism concerns us males more than ever, and so let's all be more inclusive in our efforts to achieve a better balance and become stronger together. Only then will we achieve more progress – be it curbing the scourge of domestic violence, smashing the inexplicable gender pay-gap, or ensuring greater female representation in upper echelons of establishments. These are societal issues. They are problems for *people*. If we are ever to break down boundaries of prejudice – be they racial, ethnic, sexual or other – we must find true empathy.

This new anthology, just like *Poems That Make Grown Men Cry*, is made up of diverse individuals (both contributors and poets). Their experiences are varied, their achievements multitudinous. Yet together, along with their poem selections spanning centuries, these voices evoke universal human experiences.

The common thread linking the poems in our first anthology, we found, was loss – in its many guises, be it regret, nostalgia or grief. For me, it is the common theme unifying all these new choices too. It touches us all. The rejoinder to this leveller – the *answer* to the elegiac *question* that loss poses, surely – is love.

Poetry can engender such states of grace – loss, love and true empathy – because it offers purity of emotion, much like a flood of tears. Poems provide genuine truth-to-power.

In this millennial whirl of interconnectedness, in which everyone has immediate, bite-sized opinions, we *all* sometimes need to stop and think. So please indulge my suggestion that you:

Pause. Take a breath. Look into yourself, to consider the other. Their point of view.

Let the tears flow, if need be. Whoever you are . . .

Then turn the page.

Donal Og

ANONYMOUS

→ ←

NATASCHA McELHONE

'Donal Og' is recited in John Huston's last film *The Dead*. After watching that movie as a teenager I then found the same poem in an anthology, *The Rattle Bag*, edited by Ted Hughes and Seamus Heaney. This was all pre-Google searches, of course, so it seemed like a spectacular coincidence to hear and read this poem twice in the same year, without knowing who wrote it or where it came from.

It has since become quite popular; I saw it in the literary supplement of a newspaper and then heard it read beautifully on Roger McGough's Radio 4 programme *Poetry Please*.

I still find it just as affecting now as I did at sixteen. More so, in fact.

Donal Og

It is late last night the dog was speaking of you;
the snipe was speaking of you in her deep marsh.
It is you are the lonely bird through the woods;
and that you may be without a mate until you find me.

You promised me, and you said a lie to me,
that you would be before me where the sheep are flocked;
I gave a whistle and three hundred cries to you,
and I found nothing there but a bleating lamb.

You promised me a thing that was hard for you,
a ship of gold under a silver mast;
twelve towns with a market in all of them,
and a fine white court by the side of the sea.

You promised me a thing that is not possible,
that you would give me gloves of the skin of a fish;
that you would give me shoes of the skin of a bird;
and a suit of the dearest silk in Ireland.

When I go by myself to the Well of Loneliness,
I sit down and I go through my trouble;
when I see the world and do not see my boy,
he that has an amber shade in his hair.

It was on that Sunday I gave my love to you;
the Sunday that is last before Easter Sunday
and myself on my knees reading the Passion;
and my two eyes giving love to you for ever.

My mother has said to me not to be talking with you
    today,
or tomorrow, or on the Sunday;
it was a bad time she took for telling me that;
it was shutting the door after the house was robbed.

My heart is as black as the blackness of the sloe,
or as the black coal that is on the smith's forge;
or as the sole of a shoe left in white halls;
it was you put that darkness over my life.

You have taken the east from me, you have taken the west
    from me;
you have taken what is before me and what is behind me;
you have taken the moon, you have taken the sun from
    me;
and my fear is great that you have taken God from me!

(8th century)

TRANSLATION BY LADY AUGUSTA GREGORY

→ ←

The actress **Natascha McElhone** is known for her roles in such films as *The Devil's Own* (1997), *Ronin* (1998), *The Truman Show* (1998) and *Solaris* (2002), as well as the US television series *Californication* (2007–14). She is also the author of *After You* (2010).

Isn't That Something?
RUMI (1207–73)
→ ←

ELIF SHAFAK

I love this poem. It is very short, and perhaps simple at first glance. I sincerely believe it needs to be read twice, at least, and if possible, it needs to be read aloud. The first time, for the meaning. The second time, for the music.

This poem is singing. There is a melody in every word and a cadence in each sigh. I wonder if you hear it.

'Something in His eye grabs hold of a tambourine in me, then I turn and lift a violin in someone else . . .' says Rumi. It is as if we all carry deep inside our hearts a musical instrument waiting to be heard. The only way to tune them is through Love.

Only through the breath of love can we 'unleash the beautiful wild forces' within, like St Francis said.

There is something in this poem that makes me want to cry. It is very visual. I can almost see it unfold as I read. I see it in colours more than shapes.

I like it when words move like this, reaching from one person to another, from one stranger to the next, building verbal bridges between our minds, traversing huge distances in one short step.

We are so focused on our grand ambitions, big dreams, success plans, that sometimes we tend to forget the power of simple things in daily life.

Rumi's words open up a closed door somewhere inside your soul; the wind blows in, you shiver a little, perhaps, but you are ready for a new thought, a new worldview, a new day ... Time to discard all kinds of bigotries and hatreds.

Someone else's imagination stirs mine, and my imagination might inspire yours. We are all interconnected through invisible threads.

Time for your words to touch my silences and give them a voice.

Creativity is contagious. When I hear you sing, I am tempted to write a new story; when you read my story, your soul begins to dance, and so it goes, on and on. The journey is open-ended.

Isn't that something?

Isn't That Something?

I
like when
the music happens like this:

Something in His eye grabs hold of a
tambourine in
me,

then I turn and lift a violin in someone else,
and they turn, and this turning
continues;

it has
reached you now. Isn't that
something?

(13th century)

TRANSLATION BY DANIEL LADINSKY

✦ ✦

The Turkish writer and academic **Elif Shafak** has published four-teen books, nine of them novels, including *The Bastard of Istanbul* (2007), *The Forty Rules of Love* (2010), *Honour* (2012) and *The Architect's Apprentice* (2015). She is a Chevalier dans l'Ordre des Arts et Lettres.

Bani Adam

SA'ADI (1210–91)

→ ←

NAZANIN BONIADI

My father used to read me classical Persian mythology and poetry to sleep at night instead of lullabies. As I grew older I learned the meaning behind these profound literary works. One of my favourite poems, 'Bani Adam' by famed thirteenth-century Persian poet Sa'adi, captured the core essence of human rights and sparked my passion for activism at an early age. Its unifying message of equality is inscribed on the United Nations building entrance and continues to inspire me to this day.

بنی آدم اعضای یک پیکرند
که در آفرینش ز یک گوهرند
چو عضوی به درد آورد روزگار
دگر عضوها را نماند قرار
تو کز محنت دیگران بی غمی
نشاید که نامت نهند آدمی

Here is a simple English translation of the poem:

> The sons of Adam are limbs of each other,
> Having been created of one essence.
> When the calamity of time affects one limb
> The other limbs cannot remain at rest.
> If you have no sympathy for the troubles of others,
> You are unworthy to be called by the name of Human.

And a rhyming translation :

> Human beings are members of a whole,
> In creation of one essence and soul.
> If one member is afflicted with pain,
> Other members uneasy will remain.
> If you've no sympathy for human pain,
> The name of human you cannot retain!

(13th century)

➜ ←

The Iranian-British actress **Nazanin Boniadi** has appeared on television in such series as *How I Met Your Mother* and *Homeland*, and in several films including *Iron Man* (2008), *The Next Three Days* (2010) and *Ben-Hur* (2016).

The Angels at the Tavern Door

HAFIZ (C. 1325–90)

➜ ➜

LADAN BOROUMAND

Poetry is part of the earliest and fondest memories I have of my father. He knew thousands of verses by heart and would teach us his favourite poems. As I grew old and came to read poems in French I realized that Persian poetry is the crucible of multiple aesthetic emotions that one usually experiences separately through painting, music and literature. In this lies the secret of its dizzying beauty. Hafiz was the companion of my adolescence. I loved his calm, rebellious freedom. This ode is to man endowed by God with Truth, responsibility and the fire of love, which together make religious quarrels and disputes a nonsense.

دوش دیدم که ملائک در میخانه زدند
گل آدم بسرشتند و به پیمانه زدند
ساکنان حرم ستر و عفاف ملکوت
با من راه نشین باده ی مستانه زدند
آسمان بار امانت نتوانست کشید
قرعه ی کار به نام من دیوانه زدند
جنگ هفتاد و دو ملت همه را عذر بنه

چون دیدند حقیقت ره افسانه ندزد
شکر ازرا که به میان من و او صلح افتاد
حوریان رقص کنان ساغر شکرانه ندزد
آتش آن نیست که از شعله او خندد شمع
آتش آن است که در خرمن پروانه ندزد
کس چو حافظ نکشید از رخ اندیشه نقاب
تا سر زلف سخن را به قلم شانه ندزد

The Angels at the Tavern Door
Last night I dreamed that angels stood without
The tavern door, and knocked in vain, and wept;
They took the clay of Adam, and, methought,
Moulded a cup therewith while all men slept.
Oh dwellers in the halls of Chastity!
You brought Love's passionate red wine to me,
Down to the dust I am, your bright feet stept.

For Heaven's self was all too weak to bear
The burden of His love God laid on it,
He turned to seek a messenger elsewhere,
And in the Book of Fate my name was writ.
Between my Lord and me such concord lies
As makes the Huris glad in Paradise,
With songs of praise through the green glades they flit.

A hundred dreams of Fancy's garnered store
Assail me – Father Adam went astray
Tempted by one poor grain of corn! Wherefore
Absolve and pardon him that turns away

Though the soft breath of Truth reaches his ears,
For two-and-seventy Jangling creeds he hears,
And loud-voiced Fable calls him ceaselessly.

That, that is not the flame of Love's true fire
Which makes the torchlight shadows dance in rings,
But where the radiance draws the moth's desire
And send him forth with scorched and drooping wings.
The heart of one who dwells retired shall break,
Rememb'ring a black mole and a red cheek,
And his life ebb, sapped at its secret springs.

Yet since the earliest time that man has sought
To comb the locks of Speech, his goodly bride,
Not one, like Hafiz, from the face of Thought
Has torn the veil of Ignorance aside.

(c. 1370)

TRANSLATION BY GERTRUDE BELL

→ ←

Co-founder and research director of the Abdorrahman Boroumand
Foundation for the Promotion of Human Rights and Democracy in
Iran, **Ladan Boroumand** is the author of *La Guerre des Principes*
(1999), a study of the French Revolution's impact on human rights,
as well as studies of the Islamic revolution in Iran, and the nature
of Islamist terrorism.

Grief fills the room up
(from *King John*)
WILLIAM SHAKESPEARE (1564–1616)

➤ ✦

MARINA WARNER

Constance is one of Shakespeare's blazing female characters, whose power lies in their tongue; she rails and cajoles, raves and entreats, by turns pouring scorn from her full majestic stature and prostrating herself, whimpering. There is no form of speech from the book of rhetoric that Shakespeare conned as a boy in the grammar school in Stratford that he does not offer her. But to no avail. And her helplessness, before the ruthless power-broking of her enemies, wrings the heart. For unlike other honey-tongued girls and women in the plays (Portia, Viola, Rosalind, Imogen), when Constance lets flow her torrents of words to fight for her son Arthur, she fails. Her astonishing personification of grief as a living being, the future ghost of the son she knows is doomed, comes at the end of a protracted tangled scene of struggle which ends with her utter defeat.

The fierce love of Constance for her boy, her sense of the danger he is in, and his innocent trustfulness, take *King John* far beyond its historical setting and make it speak directly to us, now, about the deepest emotions and terrors. Constance is a queen, but she is any woman with a child in danger; he is a prince but also one of Shakespeare's tender golden boys and girls who, like chimney sweepers, must come to dust.

Act Three, Scene Four

Grief fills the room up of my absent child,
Lies in his bed, walks up and down with me,
Puts on his pretty looks, repeats his words,
Remembers me of all his gracious parts,
Stuffs out his vacant garments with his form;
Then, have I reason to be fond of grief?
Fare you well: had you such a loss as I,
I could give better comfort than you do.
I will not keep this form upon my head,
When there is such disorder in my wit.
O Lord! my boy, my Arthur, my fair son!
My life, my joy, my food, my all the world!
My widow-comfort, and my sorrows' cure!

(1596)

→ ←

The writer **Marina Warner** is known for her work in mythology and feminism. Her many books range from *Alone of All Her Sex: The Cult of the Virgin Mary* (1976) to *Stranger Magic: Charmed States and the Arabian Nights* (2011). Professor of English and Creative Writing at Birkbeck, University of London, she was appointed DBE in 2015.

Extract from *The Duchess of Malfi*

JOHN WEBSTER (C. 1580–1634)

→ ←

JANET SUZMAN

What humanity, bravery, lack of self-pity this woman shows here. And threaded through all those virtues a kind of ironical common sense that is breathtaking. I can't think of anyone in fiction who meets their end with as much grace. Oh well, maybe Cleopatra does, and maybe anarchic Hedda does, in taking their own lives . . . but not with the unmatched language of this angry, desolated, misjudged woman whose vibrant life is about to be quenched by villains far, far beneath her in quality. She finds herself eager to be out of their filthy company forever. Her courage and her pride make one want to both weep for her and applaud her all at once.

From *The Duchess of Malfi*

Not a whit:
What would it pleasure me to have my throat cut
With diamonds? or to be smothered
With cassia? or to be shot to death with pearls?
I know death hath ten thousand several doors
For men to take their exits: and 'tis found

They go on such strange geometrical hinges,
You may open them both ways; any way, for Heaven's
    sake,
So I were out of your whispering. Tell my brothers
That I perceive death, now I am well awake,
Best gift is they can give, or I can take.
I would fain put off my last woman's fault,
I'd not be tedious to you.

(1612–13)

→ ←

The South African-born actress and director **Janet Suzman** played many leading roles with the Royal Shakespeare Company before turning to Ibsen, Chekhov, Pinter, Fugard, et al. Her films include *Nicholas and Alexandra* (1971), *The Draughtsman's Contract* (1982), Fellini's *And the Ship Sails On* (1983) and *A Dry White Season* (1989). She directed the boycott-breaking Johannesburg *Othello* for The Market Theatre in 1987 and has adapted and directed plays by Brecht and Chekhov relocated to the new South Africa. Her most recent book *Not Hamlet* meditates on roles for women. She was appointed DBE in 2011.

On My First Son

BEN JONSON (1572–1637)

→ ←

KATHERINE BUCKNELL

I don't feel Jonson is trying to move me; he is using all his art to control his own sorrow and rage at losing his seven-year-old son to the plague, a son he liked as well as loved. He speaks to his boy so gently, in one or two-syllable words any child could understand, with predictable rhymes. Suddenly, he releases an adult exhalation of pain, like a sob, 'O, could I lose all father now,' expressing his wish never to have been a father at all. Imagine commas around the word 'father', and the line becomes even darker, a plea directly to God: 'O, could I lose all, Father . . .' Benjamin means son of the right hand, and the right hand is where Christ sits beside his divine Father in heaven. The poem plays on this idea that Benjamin was only loaned, like Christ. Reading aloud, my voice always catches at 'Rest in soft peace'. We hope this for our children, each time we swaddle them, rock them, lay them in their cots. But we cannot protect them; in some things we are as helpless as they.

Jonson was a Christian; heaven as a better place than earth was not a sentimental euphemism for him, but consider that his own father died before Jonson was born, that he offered Benjamin love he himself had never received, and his indignation and scepticism are understandable. So 'Here doth lie' is perhaps a pun. Reading through the enjambement into the next line, the meaning could be: here is the grave of the best thing Jonson ever made. And the meaning could also be: here is the best lie Jonson ever wrote, this piece of poetry feigning calm, resignation to God's will, and any feeling that Benjamin has gone to a better place.

On My First Son

Farewell, thou child of my right hand, and joy;
My sin was too much hope of thee, lov'd boy.
Seven years tho' wert lent to me, and I thee pay,
Exacted by thy fate, on the just day.
O, could I lose all father now! For why
Will man lament the state he should envy?
To have so soon 'scap'd world's and flesh's rage,
And if no other misery, yet age?
Rest in soft peace, and, ask'd, say, 'Here doth lie
Ben Jonson his best piece of poetry.'
For whose sake henceforth all his vows be such,
As what he loves may never like too much.

(1616)

→ ←

Katherine Bucknell is an American writer based in London. She is the editor of W. H. Auden's *Juvenilia* and four volumes of the diaries of Christopher Isherwood, as well as *The Animals: Love Letters Between Christopher Isherwood and Don Bachardy*. She has also published four novels: *Canarino* (2004), *Leninsky Prospekt* (2005), *What You Will* (2007) and *+1* (2013).

Clerk Saunders

ANONYMOUS

➤ ◄

DIANA ATHILL

I like all ballads, but mostly they are too grimly of their time and place to engage one emotionally. 'Clerk Saunders' is, to me, an exception, first because of the wonderful directness of the first two verses, and second, because five of the seven brothers who catch the pair in bed respond with a gentle humanity quite unusual in the genre, and so does Margaret's father, who is going to comfort her, not punish her. When the dead Saunders appears at her window the poem does slip back into its own time and place, but once poor Saunders is in his grave, he too becomes gentle and humane, accepting that she may find another love eventually, just hoping it won't be as strong as theirs. I'm sure all early ballads are based on actual happenings, but this one also involves people like me.

Clerk Saunders
Clerk Saunders and may Margaret
Walk'd owre yon garden green;
And deep and heavy was the love
That fell thir twa between.

'A bed. a bed,' Clerk Saunders said,
'A bed for you and me!"
'Fye na, fye na.' said may Margaret,
'Till anes we married be!'

'Then I'll take the sword frae my scabbard
And slowly lift the pin;
And you may swear, and save your aith,
Ye ne'er let Clerk Saunders in.

'Take you a napkin in your hand,
And tie up baith your bonny e'en,
And you may swear, and save your aith,
Ye saw me na since late yestereen.'

It was about the midnight hour,
When they asleep were laid,
When in and came her seven brothers,
Wi' torches burning red;

When in and came her seven brothers,
Wi' torches burning bright;
They said, 'We hae but one sister,
And behold her lying with a knight!'

Then out and spake the first o' them,
'I bear the sword shall gar him die.'
And out and spake the second o' them,
'His father has nae mair but he.'

And out and spake the third o' them,
'I wot that they are lovers dear.'
And out and spake the fourth o' them,
'They have been in love this many a year.'

Then out and spake the fifth o' them,
'It were great sin true love to twain.'
And out and spake the sixth o' them,
'It were shame to slay a sleeping man.'

Then up and gat the seventh o' them,
And never a word spake he;
But he has striped his bright brown brand
Out through Clerk Saunders' fair bodye.

Clerk Saunders he started, and Margaret she turn'd
Into his arms as asleep she lay;
And sad and silent was the night
That was atween their twae.

And they lay still and sleepit sound
Until the day began to daw';
And kindly she to him did say,
'It is time, true love, you were awa'.'

But he lay still and sleepit sound,
Albeit the sun began to sheen;
She look'd atween her and the wa',
And dull and drowsie were his e'en.

Then in and came her father dear;
Said, 'Let a' your mourning be;
I'll carry the dead corse to the clay,
And I'll come back and comfort thee.'

'Comfort weel your seven sons,
For comforted I will never be;
I ween 'twas neither knave nor loon
Was in the bower last night wi' me.'

The clinking bell gaed through the town,
To carry the dead corse to the clay;
And Clerk Saunders stood at may Margaret's window,
I wot, an hour before the day.

'Are ye sleeping, Marg'ret?' he says,
'Or are ye waking presentlie?
Give me my faith and troth again,
I wot, true love, I gied to thee.'

'Your faith and troth ye sall never get,
Nor our true love sall never twin,
Until ye come within my bower,
And kiss me cheik and chin.'

'My mouth it is fill cold, Marg'ret;
It has the smell, now, of the ground;
And if I kiss thy comely mouth,
Thy days of life will not be lang.

'O cocks are crowing a merry midnight;
I wot the wild fowls are boding day;
Give me my faith and troth again,
And let me fare on my way.'

'They faith and troth thou sallna get,
And our true love sall never twin,
Until ye tell what comes o' women,
I wot, who die in strong traivelling?'

'Their beds are made in the heaven high,
Down at the foot of our good Lord's knee,
Weel set about wi' gillyflowers;
I wot, sweet company for to see.

'O cockes are crowing a merry midnight;
I wot the wild fowls are boding day;
The psalms of heaven will soon be sung,
And I, ere now, will be miss'd away.'

Then she has taken a crystal wand,
And she has stroken her troth thereon;
She has given it him at the shot-window,
Wi' mony a sad sigh and heavy groan.

'I thank ye, Marg'ret; I thank ye, Marg'ret;
And ay I thank ye heartilie;
Gin ever the dead come for the quick;
Be sure, Marg'ret, I'll come for thee.'

It's hosen and shoon, and gown alone,
She climb'd the wall and follow'd him,
Until she came to the green forest,
And there she lost the sight o' him.

'Is there ony room at your head, Saunders?
Is there ony room at your feet?
Or ony room at your side, Saunders?
Where fain, fain, I wad sleep?'

'There's nae room at my head, Marg'ret,
There's nae room at my feet;
My bed it is fu' lowly now,
Amang the hungry worms I sleep.

'Cauld mould is my covering now,
But and my winding-sheet,
The dew it falls nae sooner down
Than my resting-place is weet.

'But plait a wand o' bonny birk,
And lay it on my breast;
And shed a tear upon my grave,
And wish my saul gude rest.'

Then up and crew the cock, red cock,
And up and crew the gray,
''Tis time, 'tis time, my dear Marg'ret,
That you were going away.

'And fair Marg'ret, and rare Marg'ret,
And Marg'ret o' veritie,
Gin e'er ye love another man,
Ne'er love him as ye did me.'

(c. 17th century)

→ ←

Diana Athill was a founding director of the British publishing firm of André Deutsch, where for fifty years she worked with writers including Jean Rhys, Stevie Smith, Margaret Atwood, Molly Keane, Jack Kerouac, John Updike, Norman Mailer and Philip Roth. She has published a novel, collections of stories and letters, and seven volumes of memoirs, including a study of old age, *Somewhere Towards the End*, which won the 2008 Costa Award, and *Alive, Alive Oh!* (2015).

Frost at Midnight

SAMUEL TAYLOR COLERIDGE (1772–1834)

→ ←

HELEN MACDONALD

Two things are guaranteed to make me cry. One is *Field of Dreams*. That's Kevin Costner, love, death, baseball and forgiveness. The other is this, such a classic poem of literary Romanticism it seems wrong to mention it in the same breath as a baseball movie. The setting is Coleridge's cottage on a winter's night, his son sleeping by his side. Here is a father musing over the future life of his beloved child. But here also is a meditation on solitude, on the complicated workings of thought, memory, imagination, hope, nature, education, selfhood and Spirit. 'Stranger' was the traditional name for the fluttering film of ash on a dying fire; it was thought to portend the arrival of a friend. Here the poet accords life and meaning to this inanimate entity, making it a companionable thing. So do we all, in our various ways, unconsciously project our needs onto the things around us. 'Frost at Midnight' is a poem of solitude that works hard against all our lonelinesses. *Therefore*, the word which gathers up the poem in a burst of conviction, love and hope – that is the moment where the world turns. Look, I'm weeping even now.

Frost at Midnight

The Frost performs its secret ministry,
Unhelped by any wind. The owlet's cry
Came loud – and hark, again! loud as before.
The inmates of my cottage, all at rest,
Have left me to that solitude, which suits
Abstruser musings: save that at my side
My cradled infant slumbers peacefully.
'Tis calm indeed! so calm, that it disturbs
And vexes meditation with its strange
And extreme silentness. Sea, hill, and wood,
This populous village! Sea, and hill, and wood,
With all the numberless goings-on of life,
Inaudible as dreams! the thin blue flame
Lies on my low-burnt fire, and quivers not;
Only that film, which fluttered on the grate,
Still flutters there, the sole unquiet thing.
Methinks, its motion in this hush of nature
Gives it dim sympathies with me who live,
Making it a companionable form,
Whose puny flaps and freaks the idling Spirit
By its own moods interprets, every where
Echo or mirror seeking of itself,
And makes a toy of Thought.

But O! how oft,
How oft, at school, with most believing mind,
P⸺, have I gazed upon the bars,
⸺hat fluttering *stranger*! and as oft
⸺sed lids, already had I dreamt
⸺birth-place, and the old church-tower,

MS THAT MAKE GROWN WOMEN CRY

Whose bells, the poor man's only music, rang
From morn to evening, all the hot Fair-day,
So sweetly, that they stirred and haunted me
With a wild pleasure, falling on mine ear
Most like articulate sounds of things to come!
So gazed I, till the soothing things, I dreamt,
Lulled me to sleep, and sleep prolonged my dreams!
And so I brooded all the following morn,
Awed by the stern preceptor's face, mine eye
Fixed with mock study on my swimming book:
Save if the door half opened, and I snatched
A hasty glance, and still my heart leaped up,
For still I hoped to see the *stranger's* face,
Townsman, or aunt, or sister more beloved,
My play-mate when we both were clothed alike!

Dear Babe, that sleepest cradled by my side,
Whose gentle breathings, heard in this deep calm,
Fill up the interspersèd vacancies
And momentary pauses of the thought!
My babe so beautiful! it thrills my heart
With tender gladness, thus to look at thee,
And think that thou shalt learn far other lore,
And in far other scenes! For I was reared
In the great city, pent 'mid cloisters dim,
And saw nought lovely but the sky and stars.
But *thou*, my babe! shalt wander like a breeze
By lakes and sandy shores, beneath the crags
Of ancient mountain, and beneath the clouds,
Which image in their bulk both lakes and shores
And mountain crags: so shalt thou see and hear

The lovely shapes and sounds intelligible
Of that eternal language, which thy God
Utters, who from eternity doth teach
Himself in all, and all things in himself.
Great universal Teacher! he shall mould
Thy spirit, and by giving make it ask.

    Therefore all seasons shall be sweet to thee,
Whether the summer clothe the general earth
With greenness, or the redbreast sit and sing
Betwixt the tufts of snow on the bare branch
Of mossy apple-tree, while the nigh thatch
Smokes in the sun-thaw; whether the eave-drops fall
Heard only in the trances of the blast,
Or if the secret ministry of frost
Shall hang them up in silent icicles,
Quietly shining to the quiet Moon.

(1798)

➚ ➛

The English naturalist, writer and broadcaster **Helen Macdonald** won the Samuel Johnson Prize and Costa Book of the Year 2014 for *H is for Hawk*, her bestselling chronicle of a year spent training a goshawk. Her previous books include *Shaler's Fish* (2001) and *Falcon* (2006). She is an affiliated research scholar at the University of Cambridge's Department of History and Philosophy of Science.

I loved the Boy . . .

WILLIAM WORDSWORTH (1770–1850)

➜ ←

PAM AYRES

This is not strictly a poem, but an excerpt from a letter. It was written on 1 December 1812 by William Wordsworth, following the death of his six-year-old son from measles. I first saw it recently, included in the Order of Service at the funeral of a fine young man I knew. It is most certainly a poem to me.

I loved the Boy . . .
I loved the Boy with the utmost love
Of which my soul is capable,
And he is taken from me –
Yet in the agony of my spirit
In surrendering such a treasure
I feel a thousand times richer
Than if I had never possessed it.

(1812)

➜ ←

The performance poet **Pam Ayres** has published eight volumes of poetry, from *Some of Me Poems* (1976) to *You Made Me Late Again!* (2013).

So, we'll go no more a roving
LORD BYRON (1788–1824)
➤ ◄

JUDI DENCH

My late husband Michael Williams and I used to do a lot of recitals, many of them with Robert Spencer. Halfway through the recital, Robert would recite this poem, and it always reduced me to tears, so much so that I was incapable of continuing the recital if it was my turn next. As a result, we changed the order so that Michael followed this particular piece and I had time to compose myself.

EMILY MORTIMER

Lord Byron was my father's favourite poet and pin-up. My sister Rosie and I read this poem at his funeral. Our dad was eighty-five when he died. He never gave up trying to be young at heart. But it was a constant battle: 'old age is not for sissies' he'd say. This poem is a perfect meditation on youth ceding to age. It's sad and accepting and beautifully melancholic but I think it's a little bit hopeful too. You can still sense the twinkle in Byron's eye. The feeling that, despite all appearances to the contrary, while there's life there's hope. That there might just be one more chance for a bit of roving – even if the roving is only possible in our heads and hearts. My dad was definitely still roving in his head and in his heart until the day he died. The poem makes me cry because it reminds me of my father and makes me wish he were still here.

So, we'll go no more a roving

So, we'll go no more a roving
    So late into the night,
Though the heart be still as loving,
    And the moon be still as bright.

For the sword outwears its sheath,
    And the soul wears out the breast,
And the heart must pause to breathe,
    And love itself have rest.

Though the night was made for loving,
    And the day returns too soon,
Yet we'll go no more a roving
    By the light of the moon.

(1817)

➔ ←

In a career spanning seven decades, **Judi Dench** has been hailed both for her work onstage, including roles for the Royal Shakespeare Company and the National Theatre, and onscreen, notably *Mrs Brown* (1997), *Shakespeare in Love* (1998), *Chocolat* (2000), *Iris* (2001), *Notes on a Scandal* (2006), *Philomena* (2013), and M in seven James Bond films from *Goldeneye* (1995) to *Skyfall* (2012). She has won an Academy Award, ten BAFTAs and a record six

Olivier Awards. She was appointed DBE in 1988 and was made a Companion of Honour in 2005.

→ ←

The actress and writer **Emily Mortimer** is known for her roles in films such as *Lovely & Amazing* (2001), *Match Point* (2005), *The Pink Panther* (2006), *Lars and the Real Girl* (2007), *Shutter Island* (2010) and *Hugo* (2011). Her television credits include *30 Rock*, *The Newsroom* and *Doll & Em*, which she also co-created and wrote with Dolly Wells.

Ode to a Nightingale

JOHN KEATS (1795–1821)

➔ ✦

MARINA LEWYCKA

I first read 'Ode to a Nightingale' when I was studying for my A-levels, seventeen years old, and boiling over with teenage angst, boyfriend troubles, acne and rebellion. Here was a poem, I thought, that spoke directly to me; it seemed to whisk me out of the stuffy classroom, out of the dull suburban home where I lived with my parents, and into the magical 'embalmed darkness', where I could lose myself in the 'verdurous glooms and winding mossy ways', flirt with alcohol and mild hallucinogens, and surrender to the ecstasy of music. I read it and I wept.

Now many years later, having known real grief – the deaths of my parents, illnesses and deaths of dear precious friends snatched away far too soon – I find the tears don't flow nearly as readily as they did when I was seventeen. It's as though real grief has shamed away the easy tears of adolescence. A small bossy voice inside my head tells me that now I'm a grown woman tears are an idle luxury and there are many people in this world with much more to cry about than me. Yet often in my heart I know that nothing would make me feel better so much as a good cry. And that's when I reach for Keats's 'Ode to a Nightingale'.

John Keats was just twenty-three when he wrote this poem in 1819, closer in age to my adolescent self than to my 'grown woman' self, but in experience already an adult on familiar terms with death. His beloved brother Tom had just died of consumption, 'pale and spectre thin', and he himself was infected with the same disease. He died painfully two years later, disappointed in love, his poetry unrecognized, and without ever knowing the extent of the fame he would posthumously enjoy. The natural world whose sensual beauty he celebrated – 'The coming musk-rose, full of dewy wine, / The murmurous haunt of flies on summer eves' – was as indifferent to his greatness as he, in death, would be to the nightingale's requiem: I read it and I weep.

Ode to a Nightingale

My heart aches, and a drowsy numbness pains
    My sense, as though of hemlock I had drunk,
Or emptied some dull opiate to the drains
    One minute past, and Lethe-wards had sunk:
'Tis not through envy of thy happy lot,
    But being too happy in thine happiness, –
      That thou, light-wingèd Dryad of the trees,
      In some melodious plot
Of beechen green, and shadows numberless,
    Singest of summer in full-throated ease.

Oh, for a draught of vintage, that hath been
    Cooled a long age in the deep-delvèd earth,
Tasting of Flora and the country green,
    Dance, and Provençal song, and sunburnt mirth!

Oh for a beaker full of the warm South,
        Full of the true, the blushful Hippocrene,
            With beaded bubbles winking at the brim,
                And purple-stainèd mouth,
That I might drink, and leave the world unseen,
        And with thee fade away into the forest dim:

Fade far away, dissolve, and quite forget
        What thou among the leaves hast never known,
The weariness, the fever, and the fret
        Here, where men sit and hear each other groan;
Where palsy shakes a few, sad, last gray hairs,
        Where youth grows pale, and spectre-thin, and dies;
            Where but to think is to be full of sorrow
                And leaden-eyed despairs;
Where Beauty cannot keep her lustrous eyes,
        Or new Love pine at them beyond to-morrow.

Away! away! for I will fly to thee,
        Not charioted by Bacchus and his pards,
But on the viewless wings of Poesy,
        Though the dull brain perplexes and retards:
Already with thee! Tender is the night,
        And haply the Queen-Moon is on her throne,
            Clustered around by all her starry Fays;
                But here there is no light,
Save what from heaven is with the breezes blown
        Through verdurous glooms and winding
        mossy ways.

I cannot see what flowers are at my feet,
      Nor what soft incense hangs upon the boughs,
But, in embalmèd darkness, guess each sweet
      Wherewith the seasonable month endows
The grass, the thicket, and the fruit-tree wild;
      White hawthorn, and the pastoral eglantine;
            Fast-fading violets covered up in leaves;
                  And mid-May's eldest child,
The coming musk-rose, full of dewy wine,
      The murmurous haunt of flies on summer eves.

Darkling, I listen; and, for many a time
      I have been half in love with easeful Death,
Called him soft names in many a musèd rhyme,
      To take into the air my quiet breath;
Now more than ever seems it rich to die,
      To cease upon the midnight with no pain,
            While thou art pouring forth thy soul abroad
                  In such an ecstasy!
      Still wouldst thou sing, and I have ears in vain –
            To thy high requiem become a sod.

Thou wast not born for death, immortal bird!
      No hungry generations tread thee down;
The voice I hear this passing night was heard
      In ancient days by emperor and clown:
Perhaps the self-same song that found a path
      Through the sad heart of Ruth, when, sick for home,
            She stood in tears amid the alien corn;
                  The same that oft-times hath

Charm'd magic casements, opening on the foam
    Of perilous seas, in faery lands forlorn.

Forlorn! The very word is like a bell
    To toll me back from thee to my sole self.
Adieu! The fancy cannot cheat so well
    As she is famed to do, deceiving elf,
Adieu! adieu! Thy plaintive anthem fades
    Past the near meadows, over the still stream,
        Up the hill-side; and now 'tis buried deep
        In the next valley-glades:
    Was it a vision, or a waking dream?
        Fled is that music: – do I wake or sleep?

(1819)

→ ←

Born in Germany of Ukrainian parentage, but long based in Britain, **Marina Lewycka** won many awards for her debut novel *A Short History of Tractors in Ukrainian* (2005), which has been translated into thirty-five languages. Her subsequent books include the novels *Two Caravans* (2007), *We Are All Made of Glue* (2009), *Various Pets Alive and Dead* (2012) and *The Lubetkin Legacy* (2016).

Extract from
The Masque of Anarchy
PERCY BYSSHE SHELLEY (1792–1822)
→ ←

TENA ŠTIVIČIĆ

The first time I came across this poem I was in my late teens. It was only a cursory look, without full knowledge of the context, and in fact I probably didn't read it all the way through. But I remember that the famous passage –

> Rise like Lions after slumber
> In unvanquishable number.
> Shake your chains to earth like dew
> Which in sleep had fallen on you –
> Ye are many – they are few.

– made me well up.

My view of the world took shape in the eighties. For a child who was becoming a teenager and was forming the foundations of a belief system, the world around me was increasingly secular, prosperous and with ever increasing gender equality. Lessons had been learnt in the two world wars, we had the European Convention of

Human Rights and figures like Gandhi were within my general scope of reference. Amid the lax socialism of the eighties, Yugoslavia felt like a fairly free place to live. Yugoslavia, such as it was, guaranteed a certain minimum level of existential security. This was something I grew up taking for granted.

From *The Masque of Anarchy*
What art thou, Freedom ? O ! could slaves
Answer from their living graves
This demand – tyrants would flee
Like a dream's dim imagery :

Thou are not, as impostors say,
A shadow soon to pass away,
A superstition, and a name
Echoing from the cave of Fame.

For the labourer thou art bread,
And a comely table spread
From his daily labour come
In a neat and happy home.

Thou art clothes, and fire, and food
For the trampled multitude –
No – in countries that are free
Such starvation cannot be
As in England now we see.

(1819)

'Ye are many – they are few', the last line of the most striking passage, stirred up my emotions, for sure, but they were a mixture of empathy for humanity and pride at how far we've come. Those words were words about the past. About a time we as a species have surpassed.

I came across this poem again a couple of years ago. Quite unexpectedly, almost as an ambush, it made me cry again, but for shockingly different reasons. The nostalgia is gone. Perhaps things only seemed as though they had changed, or perhaps they took a sharp turn somewhere between those teenage years of my life and now. But today I'm living in this rampant, decadent late phase of capitalism. Today, I am part of the 99 per cent who sometimes try but seem to fail to shake the chains. Today I am astonished to find that this is a poem about the present.

> ← ←

The works of the Croatian-born playwright **Tena Štivičić**, now resident in London, have been performed in a dozen European countries, including the award-winning *Fragile!* (2005) in Slovenia and *3 Winters* at London's National Theatre (2014), for which she won the 2015 Susan Smith Blackburn Prize. Her project *Goldoni Terminus* featured at the 2007 Venice Biennale.

Ulysses

ALFRED, LORD TENNYSON (1809–92)

➤ ◂

ERICA JONG

I can't remember when I first read this poem. But the rhythms and the subject-matter have always captivated me.

Ulysses, the adventurer, has grown old and is cooling his heels on his native isle, Ithaka. He looks back at his amazing adventures sailing home from Troy with his triumphant men and he longs for youth – with all its troubles. And he has had troubles. Troubles are the price of adventure.

Yes, he won the war by introducing the brilliant decoy of the hollow wooden horse, filled with fighters. And he is home with his faithful wife Penelope and his son Telemachus to whom he leaves 'the sceptre and the isle'. But old age is boring and what son can truly understand his aged father? His son is no adventurer but rather 'centred in the sphere of common duties'. He is a good son, but uninspiring, or so Ulysses implies. 'He works his work, I mine.' Never has a father so damned a son with faint praise!

Ulysses does his duty, as does Telemachus. Yet as the poem moves toward its conclusion, we feel the unmistakable stirring of adventure, the desire to push off from Ithaka again and experience the passions of youth and discovery.

> There lies the port; the vessel puffs her sail:
> There gloom the dark broad seas.

Contemplating his own death, Ulysses sees it as a quest for adventure, a fierce desire never to yield. Perhaps he will 'touch the Happy Isles' or 'see the great Achilles, who we knew.' He dreams of being with heroes again, exploring the ends of the earth. Turning his back on dull duty, he is sailing with his crew – who are, of course, all dead like Achilles.

And yet their unyielding spirit never dies. And the poem closes with a celebration of heroism and striving. Ulysses may be old, but his spirit remains young – which is probably why we so love this poem.

Ulysses
It little profits that an idle king,
By this still hearth, among these barren crags,
Matched with an agèd wife, I mete and dole
Unequal laws unto a savage race,
That hoard, and sleep, and feed, and know not me.
I cannot rest from travel: I will drink
Life to the lees: all times I have enjoy'd
Greatly, have suffer'd greatly, both with those
That loved me, and alone; on shore, and when
Thro' scudding drifts the rainy Hyades
Vext the dim sea: I am become a name;
For always roaming with a hungry heart
Much have I seen and known; cities of men

And manners, climates, councils, governments,
Myself not least, but honour'd of them all;
And drunk delight of battle with my peers,
Far on the ringing plains of windy Troy.
I am a part of all that I have met;
Yet all experience is an arch wherethro'
Gleams that untravell'd world, whose margin fades
For ever and for ever when I move.
How dull it is to pause, to make an end,
To rust unburnish'd, not to shine in use!
As tho' to breathe were life. Life piled on life
Were all too little, and of one to me
Little remains: but every hour is saved
From that eternal silence, something more,
A bringer of new things; and vile it were
For some three suns to store and hoard myself,
And this gray spirit yearning in desire
To follow knowledge like a sinking star,
Beyond the utmost bound of human thought.

     This my son, mine own Telemachus,
To whom I leave the sceptre and the isle –
Well-loved of me, discerning to fulfil
This labour, by slow prudence to make mild
A rugged people, and thro' soft degrees
Subdue them to the useful and the good.
Most blameless is he, centred in the sphere
Of common duties, decent not to fail
In offices of tenderness, and pay
Meet adoration to my household gods,
When I am gone. He works his work, I mine.

     There lies the port; the vessel puffs her sail:

There gloom the dark broad seas. My mariners,
Souls that have toil'd, and wrought, and thought with
      me –
That ever with a frolic welcome took
The thunder and the sunshine, and opposed
Free hearts, free foreheads – you and I are old;
Old age hath yet his honour and his toil;
Death closes all: but something ere the end,
Some work of noble note, may yet be done,
Not unbecoming men that strove with Gods.
The lights begin to twinkle from the rocks:
The long day wanes: the slow moon climbs: the deep
Moans round with many voices. Come, my friends,
'Tis not too late to seek a newer world.
Push off, and sitting well in order smite
The sounding furrows; for my purpose holds
To sail beyond the sunset, and the baths
Of all the western stars, until I die.
It may be that the gulfs will wash us down:
It may be we shall touch the Happy Isles,
And see the great Achilles, whom we knew.
Tho' much is taken, much abides; and tho'
We are not now that strength which in old days
Moved earth and heaven; that which we are, we are;
One equal temper of heroic hearts,
Made weak by time and fate, but strong in will
To strive, to seek, to find, and not to yield.

(1833)

→ ←

The American writer and academic **Erica Jong** has published seven works of non-fiction, seven volumes of poetry and nine novels, from *Fear of Flying* (1973) to *Fear of Dying* (2015).

Abou Ben Adhem

LEIGH HUNT (1784–1859)
→ ←

JOAN BAEZ

My father taught me this poem. When he was old and near death I read it to him. He, who almost never cried, said, 'Gosh, my eyes are wet . . .'

Somewhere in my mind Abou Ben Adhem is my dad. Whatever struggles my father presented to me in my lifetime, he was a humble man. In the poem Abou Ben Adhem is rewarded for his goodness, though he has expected nothing. I like to think his sweet countenance would have been unaffected was he not. I know it would have been so with my father.

Abou Ben Adhem
Abou Ben Adhem (may his tribe increase!)
Awoke one night from a deep dream of peace,
And saw, within the moonlight in his room,
Making it rich, and like a lily in bloom,
An angel writing in a book of gold:
Exceeding peace had made Ben Adhem bold,
And to the presence in the room he said,

'What writest thou?' –The vision raised its head,
And with a look made of all sweet accord,
Answered, 'The names of those who love the Lord.'
'And is mine one?' said Abou. 'Nay, not so,'
Replied the angel. Abou spoke more low,
But cheerily still, and said, 'I pray thee, then,
Write me as one that loves his fellow men.'

The angel wrote, and vanished. The next night
It came again with a great wakening light,
And showed the names whom love of God had blest,
And lo! Ben Adhem's name led all the rest.

(1834)

→ ←

In a career lasting more than fifty years, the singer **Joan Baez** has released thirty-plus albums while gaining an international reputation as a political and social activist in the fields of human and civil rights, non-violence and the environment.

I Am

JOHN CLARE (1793–1864)

→ ←

HELEN PANKHURST

I learnt this poem by heart as a young teenager, and it has stayed with me ever since, pulling at my heart strings like no other.

One of the alternative titles to the poem is 'Written in a Northampton County Asylum'. Despite the undertone of madness, it is one of the most lucid poems about sadness and loneliness I have ever come across. It also belies simplistic judgments about mental illness.

I love the imagery swirling around in the poem, often continued over several lines such as the 'living sea of waking dreams' which then becomes the 'shipwreck of my life's esteems'; the poignancy of some lines: 'e'en (even) the dearest – that I loved the best / Are strange – nay, rather, stranger than the rest'. Then, after all the noise, the pain and angst, the last peaceful evocation – the poet is lying down and looking up: 'the grass below; above, the vaulted sky', a 'vaulted sky' . . . just beautiful.

I Am

I am – yet what I am none cares or knows;
My friends forsake me like a memory lost:
I am the self-consumer of my woes –
They rise and vanish in oblivious host,
Like shadows in love's frenzied stifled throes
And yet I am, and live – like vapours tossed

Into the nothingness of scorn and noise,
Into the living sea of waking dreams,
Where there is neither sense of life or joys,
But the vast shipwreck of my life's esteems;
And e'en the dearest – that I loved the best –
Are strange – nay, rather, stranger than the rest.

I long for scenes where man hath never trod
A place where woman never smiled or wept
There to abide with my Creator, God,
And sleep as I in childhood sweetly slept,
Untroubling and untroubled where I lie
The grass below – above the vaulted sky.

(1844–5)

➔ ←

Helen Pankhurst is a women's rights activist and senior advisor to CARE International, based in the UK and Ethiopia. She leads CARE's International Women's Day Walk which launches the annual Walk In Her Shoes campaign. Helen previously worked at WaterAid, Womankind Worldwide and the Agency for

Cooperation and Research in Development. She is the great-grand-daughter of Emmeline Pankhurst and granddaughter of Sylvia Pankhurst, leaders of the British suffragette movement.

Sonnets from the Portuguese: XXVIII

ELIZABETH BARRETT BROWNING (1806–61)

➜ ❮

A. L. KENNEDY

I wanted to pick a poem that might make one weep for joy – or out of confusion, or need, possibly because those would be my main causes for weeping. This is a wonderful sonnet – so physical and sexy about something which is so much about absence and the mind. But of course the mind is the place that makes sex really work and allows it to have proper weight.

On the surface this is a fluttery monologue, coy and Victorian and at least semi-defeated. Hands are touching where other hands have touched. The final lines preserve the privacy of the lovers. Beneath its surface, it's full of wonder, desire and a sense of two bodies being together in need and in letters, which I also like. Love should be a secret between lovers, whatever their circumstances. In a way, this is a poem to remember all those separated lovers, people who can't see their loves for political reasons, or because they've been forced into geographical separation, or because of imprisonment. One of the quieter horrors of prison lies in the removal of love, the absence of tenderness and privacy. A small hope to sustain us through any circumstances can be found in shared words.

Sonnets from the Portuguese

XXVIII

My letters! all dead paper, . . . mute and white! –
And yet they seem alive and quivering
Against my tremulous hands which loose the string
And let them drop down on my knee to-night.
This said, . . . he wished to have me in his sight
Once, as a friend: this fixed a day in spring
To come and touch my hand . . . a simple thing,
Yet I wept for it! – this, . . . the paper's light . . .
Said, *Dear, I love thee*; and I sank and quailed
As if God's future thundered on my past.
This said, *I am thine* – and so its ink has paled
With lying at my heart that beat too fast.
And this . . . O Love, thy words have ill availed,
If, what this said, I dared repeat at last!

(1845)

→ ←

The Scottish writer and comedian **A. L. Kennedy** has published seven novels, including *Day*, the 2007 Costa Book of the Year, as well as works of non-fiction, collections of short stories, screenplays and radio dramas.

Say not the struggle naught availeth

ARTHUR HUGH CLOUGH (1819–61)

→ ←

MARGARET DRABBLE

This poem by Arthur Hugh Clough unfailingly brings tears to my eyes. It speaks of hope, and effort, and disappointment, and perseverance. As I read it, it is a poem about social hope, about hope for humanity. Most of my political hopes have been, in my lifetime, disappointed, but this poem tells us not to lose faith. The imagery is profoundly beautiful, and reminds me of the great beaches of my childhood, of Wordsworth's immortal shore. I can feel those 'tired waves, vainly breaking', and then the flooding fullness of the sea. The double movement, the double crescendo of redemption in those last two stanzas, of sea and of light, is astonishingly affecting.

Say not the struggle naught availeth
Say not the struggle naught availeth,
The labour and the wounds are vain,
The enemy faints not, nor faileth,
And as things have been they remain.

If hopes were dupes, fears may be liars;
It may be, in yon smoke conceal'd,
Your comrades chase e'en now the fliers,
And, but for you, possess the field.

For while the tired waves, vainly breaking,
Seem here no painful inch to gain,
Far back, through creeks and inlets making,
Comes silent, flooding in, the main.

And not by eastern windows only,
When daylight comes, comes in the light;
In front the sun climbs slow, how slowly!
But westward, look, the land is bright!

(1849)

→ ←

Margaret Drabble has published eighteen novels, notably *A Summer Bird-Cage* (1962), *The Millstone* (1965) and *The Pure Gold Baby* (2013). She has also written one volume of short stories and several works of non-fiction, including studies of Wordsworth, Arnold Bennett and Angus Wilson. She edited two editions of the *Oxford Companion to English Literature* (1985, 2000). She was appointed DBE in 2008.

The Charge of the Light Brigade

ALFRED, LORD TENNYSON (1809–92)

➤ ✦

WENDY COPE

Quite a few of my favourite poems make me cry, especially when I try to read them aloud.

In the run-up to any event in which I'm going to read other people's poems, I practise at home to make sure I can get through them without blubbing. I have never yet managed it with 'The Charge of the Light Brigade'. Once, when I had chosen it for a radio programme, I had to ask the presenter to read it for me. Another time, at an event at Christie's, I spoke about the revisions in Tennyson's manuscript. Then my partner kindly stepped in and read the poem.

It was a favourite of my father's. He knew it by heart and often recited it. But that isn't the only reason I find it so moving. It is a wonderfully stirring poem, justly famous and popular. Imagine being the mother or sister of a young man who had lost his life because 'someone had blundered'. Imagine reading a poem insisting that, even so, his bravery and sacrifice deserved to be celebrated. I think it might have helped.

The Charge of the Light Brigade

Half a league, half a league,
    Half a league onward,
All in the valley of Death
    Rode the six hundred.
'Forward, the Light Brigade!
Charge for the guns!' he said:
Into the valley of Death
    Rode the six hundred.

'Forward, the Light Brigade!'
Was there a man dismay'd?
Not tho' the soldier knew
    Someone had blunder'd:
Theirs not to make reply,
Theirs not to reason why,
Theirs but to do and die:
Into the valley of Death
    Rode the six hundred.

Cannon to right of them,
Cannon to left of them,
Cannon in front of them
    Volley'd and thunder'd;
Storm'd at with shot and shell,
Boldly they rode and well,
Into the jaws of Death,
Into the mouth of Hell
    Rode the six hundred.

Flash'd all their sabres bare,
Flash'd as they turn'd in air,
Sabring the gunners there,
Charging an army, while
      All the world wonder'd:
Plunged in the battery-smoke
Right thro' the line they broke;
Cossack and Russian
Reel'd from the sabre stroke
      Shatter'd and sunder'd.
Then they rode back, but not,
      Not the six hundred.

Cannon to right of them,
Cannon to left of them,
Cannon behind them
      Volley'd and thunder'd;
Storm'd at with shot and shell,
While horse and hero fell,
They that had fought so well
Came thro' the jaws of Death,
Back from the mouth of Hell,
All that was left of them,
      Left of six hundred.

When can their glory fade?
O the wild charge they made!
    All the world wonder'd.
Honour the charge they made!
Honour the Light Brigade,
    Noble six hundred!

                             (1854)

➜ ⬅

Wendy Cope has published four collections of adult poetry, *Making Cocoa for Kingsley Amis* (1986), *Serious Concerns* (1992), *If I Don't Know* (2001) and *Family Values* (2011). She has also written two books of poetry for children, and edited several anthologies, including *Is That the New Moon? Poems by Women Poets* (2002) and *George Herbert: Verse and Prose* (2003).

Facing West from California's Shores

WALT WHITMAN (1819–92)

→ ←

IRMA KURTZ

Wanderlust is a serious affliction of the soul which was transported to America by the early settlers. As the condition of Wanderlust was passed down through the generations it became weaker; however when I was at university in the 1950s the travel bug was still up and kicking, sailing and hitch-hiking, if not yet flying absolutely everywhere. It so happens, mine was the same university attended by Jack Kerouac and others who were attacked by Wanderlust.

To hit the road can appease the condition only as long as the journey lasts, for to this day no matter how alluring born travellers imagine their unknown destination to be, it is the journey itself that drives them. When I read Walt Whitman's poetry as a teenager, I did not know how close to my bone his music struck, not until a day in my early thirties when I found myself standing on a beach north of San Diego. Wanderlust, which used to send most Americans westward across their vast and varied land, had a decade earlier sent this young Yank perversely eastward, first all around Europe, settling briefly there and finally here, until in due course

I journeyed to central and eastern Asia and then from Australia across the Pacific in what Americans would even now consider an eccentric route for one born on the east coast of their homeland to get herself to California for the very first time.

There in the fireworks of a Pacific sunset I took a paperback copy of selections from Whitman's *Leaves of Grass* out of my bag; it fell open to the poem 'Facing West from California's Shores'. I wept to read it then. And it brings tears to my eyes whenever I read it now that I am drawing close to the end of the journey.

Facing West from California's Shores

Facing west from California's shores,
Inquiring, tireless, seeking what is yet unfound,
I, a child, very old, over waves, towards the house of
    maternity, the land of migrations, look afar,
Look off the shores of my Western Sea, the circle almost
    circled;
For, starting westward from Hindustan, from the vales of
    Kashmere,
From Asia, from the north, from the God, the sage, and
    the hero,
From the south, from the flowery peninsulas, and the
    spice islands,
Long having wander'd since, round the earth having
    wander'd,
Now I face home again, very pleas'd and joyous,
(But where is what I started for, so long ago?
And why is it yet unfound?)

                                                    (1860)

→ ←

'Agony aunt' of *Cosmopolitan* magazine since 1973, New Jersey-born, London-based **Irma Kurtz** has made documentary series for the BBC and Channel 4 as well as writing three self-help manuals, three travel books, two novels and a memoir, *My Life in Agony* (2014).

After great pain, a formal feeling comes –

EMILY DICKINSON (1830–86)

→ ←

SIRI HUSTVEDT

No 'I' speaks in this poem. There is no whole self. The pain is in the past, but the paralysis of shock and grief are present, personified in Nerves that sit, and a Heart that questions, as if these two internal body parts have slid into their pews at a funeral to take part in a ritual for the dead. Inner life has collapsed into empty, external gestures, and time makes no sense: a day, a century? The Feet move like the limbs of a vacant automaton, and on what ground? That too has no solidity. It might be air or nothing. And then Dickinson moves from the Wooden way to Quartz to stone to Lead, one substance heavier than the next, as if to give the reader the full weight of this terrible benumbed, frozen state. Long ago, I memorized this poem. After I say the words 'Hour of Lead', tears are in my eyes. Then I am lying in the snow, and by the time I have arrived at the poem's final words 'letting go', my tears fall. It is as if the poet has given me permission, has said, Weep now. It is all right to weep now.

After great pain, a formal feeling comes –
After great pain, a formal feeling comes –
The Nerves sit ceremonious, like Tombs –
The stiff Heart questions was it He, that bore,
And Yesterday, or Centuries before?

The Feet, mechanical go round –
Of Ground, or Air, or Ought –
A Wooden way
Regardless grown,
A Quartz contentment, like a stone –

This is the Hour of Lead –
Remembered, if outlived,
As Freezing persons, recollect the snow –
First – Chill – then Stupor – then the letting go –

(c. 1862)

→ ←

The American writer **Siri Hustvedt** has published a collection of poetry, three volumes of essays, a work of non-fiction and six novels, including *What I Loved* (2003), *The Sorrows of an American* (2008) and *The Blazing World* (2014).

I took my Power in my Hand

EMILY DICKINSON (1830–86)

→ ←

ELENA FERRANTE

At times I've read these lines as a reflection on women's writing, at times as a symbol of any female venture. The first painful fact is that Dickinson has no models of her own sex to refer to, nothing, anyway, that has the aura of David. This is the source of the inevitable comparison with the male figure from the Bible. His hand is bigger, the Power at his disposal is bigger. As a result, Dickinson, in order to make an equivalent gesture, needs twice the boldness. But what's the use of being bolder? The woman who takes aim and throws her stone does not confront simply the Goliath of the youth with the slingshot: her Goliath is the entire world. Thus that throw can only be ineffectual, its sole victim the thrower. And so we arrive at the wonderful last two lines. Is the Goliath of the audacious Emily 'too large' or is it that she is 'too small'? That adjective, followed by the question mark, moves me. I wish all Emilys not to be small by nature, I wish they would just try, and try again, and so become large.

TRANSLATION BY ANN GOLDSTEIN

I took my Power in my Hand

I took my Power in my Hand –
And went against the World –
'Twas not so much as David – had –
But I – was twice as bold –

I aimed my Pebble – but Myself
Was all the one that fell –
Was it Goliath – was too large –
Or was myself – too small?

(c. 1862)

→ ←

True to her belief that 'books, once they are written, have no need of their authors', the Naples-born writer **Elena Ferrante** has stayed resolutely out of public view. She is the author of *The Days of Abandonment* (2005), *Troubling Love* (2006) and *The Lost Daughter* (2008). Her Neapolitan novels include *My Brilliant Friend* (2011), *The Story of a New Name* (2012), *Those Who Leave and Those Who Stay* (2014) and *The Story of the Lost Child* (2015). She is also the author of *Fragments* (2016), a collection of writings on reading, writing and absence.

The World – feels Dusty

EMILY DICKINSON (1830–86)

➔ ⤙

JOYCE DIDONATO

At college, as an eager Music major and sheltered Midwesterner, I was assigned a handful of songs from Aaron Copland's iconic *Twelve Poems of Emily Dickinson* for my junior recital, and I worked valiantly, if a bit in vain, to give meaning to the slightly distant, grown-up lyrics.

Nearly two decades and twenty countries later, I hovered over my father's deathbed, trying to reconcile the violent battle within me to both move the stubborn hands of the clock forward in useless effort to alleviate his suffering, while yearning to forcefully stop them from ever pushing ahead in selfish hopes to keep that moment frozen in time: the moment when he was still here. When he was still in my life.

In that moment, Emily's knowing, tranquil, perfectly simple lines flooded into my heart, as I realized the singular, golden moment at hand: the opportunity to Minister to the thirsty man (one never interested in Flags or Honours) who had brought me into this world, in his Dusty moment of release. To this day, I don't know if I helped him in that moment or not, for the pain never seemed to take leave of him, however the calm of her assuring metre makes me hope that I did.

Today this poem takes me back with tears to my father's bedside, as well as forward to mine, where I dare to hope that someone will be there for me when my Thirst comes.

The World – feels Dusty

The World – feels Dusty
When We stop to Die –
We want the Dew – then –
Honors – taste dry –

Flags – vex a Dying face –
But the least Fan
Stirred by a friend's Hand –
Cools – like the Rain –

Mine be the Ministry
When thy Thirst comes –
* And Hybla Balms –
Dews of Thessaly, to fetch –

(c. 1863)

* In the Aaron Copland arrangements of twelve of Dickinson's poems, I first encountered this poem to read:

And Holy Balms –
Dews of Thyself, to fetch –

Scholars think he may have pulled it from an earlier version, or simply misread her handwriting, as he was working from her manuscripts.

→ ←

Kansas-born mezzo-soprano **Joyce DiDonato** has appeared across the globe in operas by Rossini, Handel and Mozart. Her discography includes the Grammy-Award-winning *Diva Divo*, *Drama Queens*, *ReJoyce!* and *Stella di Napoli*. Her many other honours include the 2012 Grammy Award for Best Classical Vocal Solo, the Gramophone Artist of the Year and an induction into the Gramophone Hall of Fame. In 2015 she was elected to the Board of Trustees of Carnegie Hall, New York.

The Walrus and The Carpenter

LEWIS CARROLL (1832–98)

➔ ☙

BELLA FREUD

However funny and surrealistic this poem seems to be, there is a feeling of dread right from the start. Even though it is a nonsense poem, the atmosphere is like being in a dream with a menacing undertone which might become terrifying. But it's funny. The jokey rhythm confuses you into thinking everything is fine, meanwhile all the oysters are being lined up and sorted for annihilation. Like many cruel tyrants the Walrus is deeply sentimental, crying tears of remorse as he commits mass murder, while the Carpenter concerns himself only with the thickness of the butter on his bread. Whenever I read this poem I feel a terrible grief for the oysters.

The Walrus and The Carpenter
The sun was shining on the sea,
    Shining with all his might:
He did his very best to make
    The billows smooth and bright –
And this was odd, because it was
    The middle of the night.

The moon was shining sulkily,
         Because she thought the sun
Had got no business to be there
         After the day was done –
'It's very rude of him,' she said,
         'To come and spoil the fun.'

The sea was wet as wet could be,
         The sands were dry as dry.
You could not see a cloud, because
         No cloud was in the sky:
No birds were flying overhead –
         There were no birds to fly.

The Walrus and the Carpenter
         Were walking close at hand;
They wept like anything to see
         Such quantities of sand:
'If this were only cleared away,'
         They said, 'it would be grand!'

'If seven maids with seven mops
         Swept it for half a year,
Do you suppose,' the Walrus said,
         'That they could get it clear?'
'I doubt it,' said the Carpenter,
         And shed a bitter tear.

'O Oysters, come and walk with us!'
         The Walrus did beseech.

'A pleasant walk, a pleasant talk,
    Along the briny beach:
We cannot do with more than four,
    To give a hand to each.'

The eldest Oyster looked at him,
    But never a word he said:
The eldest Oyster winked his eye,
    And shook his heavy head –
Meaning to say he did not choose
    To leave the oyster-bed.

But four young Oysters hurried up,
    All eager for the treat:
Their coats were brushed, their faces washed,
    Their shoes were clean and neat –
And this was odd, because, you know,
    They hadn't any feet.

Four other Oysters followed them,
    And yet another four;
And thick and fast they came at last,
    And more, and more, and more –
All hopping through the frothy waves,
    And scrambling to the shore.

The Walrus and the Carpenter
    Walked on a mile or so,
And then they rested on a rock
    Conveniently low:

And all the little Oysters stood
    And waited in a row.

'The time has come,' the Walrus said,
    'To talk of many things:
Of shoes – and ships – and sealing-wax –
    Of cabbages – and kings –
And why the sea is boiling hot –
    And whether pigs have wings.'

'But wait a bit,' the Oysters cried,
    'Before we have our chat;
For some of us are out of breath,
    And all of us are fat!'
'No hurry!' said the Carpenter.
    They thanked him much for that.

'A loaf of bread,' the Walrus said,
    'Is what we chiefly need:
Pepper and vinegar besides
    Are very good indeed –
Now if you're ready, Oysters dear,
    We can begin to feed.'

'But not on us!' the Oysters cried,
    Turning a little blue.
'After such kindness, that would be
    A dismal thing to do!'
'The night is fine,' the Walrus said.
    'Do you admire the view?

'It was so kind of you to come!
  And you are very nice!'
The Carpenter said nothing but
  'Cut us another slice:
I wish you were not quite so deaf –
  I've had to ask you twice!'

'It seems a shame,' the Walrus said,
  'To play them such a trick,
After we've brought them out so far,
  And made them trot so quick!'
The Carpenter said nothing but
  'The butter's spread too thick!'

'I weep for you,' the Walrus said:
  'I deeply sympathize.'
With sobs and tears he sorted out
  Those of the largest size,
Holding his pocket-handkerchief
  Before his streaming eyes.

'O Oysters,' said the Carpenter,
  'You've had a pleasant run!
Shall we be trotting home again?'
  But answer came there none –
And this was scarcely odd, because
  They'd eaten every one.

(1871)

→ ←

Bella Freud is a London-based fashion designer. She is renowned for her graphic knits featuring the words 'Ginsberg is God', 'Je t'aime Jane' and '1970', and her designs are sold internationally. She has made eight short films, three with John Malkovich. She has recently launched a range of perfume and scented candles and the first Bella Freud standalone store is located in central London.

Life is but a Dream

LEWIS CARROLL (1832–98)

➤ ⬿

VICTORIA COREN MITCHELL

This beautiful, simple poem made me cry even when I was very young. Children have an underestimated sense of passing time, transience and nostalgia – those moods permeate all the great children's stories, particularly *Through the Looking-Glass and What Alice Found There* (which is even better than *Alice's Adventures in Wonderland*), summed up in this perfect little acrostic which appears at the end.

Life is but a Dream
A boat beneath a sunny sky,
Lingering onward dreamily
In an evening of July –

Children three that nestle near,
Eager eye and willing ear,
Pleased a simple tale to hear –

Long has paled that sunny sky:
Echoes fade and memories die.
Autumn frosts have slain July.

Still she haunts me, phantomwise,
Alice moving under skies
Never seen by waking eyes.

Children yet, the tale to hear,
Eager eye and willing ear,
Lovingly shall nestle near.

In a Wonderland they lie,
Dreaming as the days go by,
Dreaming as the summers die:

Ever drifting down the stream –
Lingering in the golden gleam –
Life, what is it but a dream?

(1865)

→ ←

The writer, broadcaster and professional poker-player **Victoria Coren Mitchell** writes several newspaper and magazine columns, and presents the BBC television quiz show *Only Connect*. She is the first poker-player to have won two European Poker Tour titles. Her books include *Once More, With Feeling: How We Tried to Make the Greatest Porn Film Ever* (2002) and *For Richer, for Poorer: A Love Affair with Poker* (2009).

When You are Old

W. B. YEATS (1865–1939)

→ ←

MARIELLA FROSTRUP

Once upon a time my interest in poetry was spurred entirely by my heartbeat. Unrequited passions and illicit desires were the heightened emotions that sped me toward poets who I felt could say precisely and concisely what I was feeling but failing to articulate. Back then, in the days when the prospect of a grey hair, let alone a headful, was both abhorrent and unimaginable, Yeats's poem was a curiosity, a glimpse into a world as alien to me as the planets silently spinning in the cosmos.

Now, many decades later, he speaks directly to my secret soul, the dignity of his enduring emotion stirring romantic impulses buried deep. Some of us are slow learners when it comes to recognizing love that is nourishing and good, that smooths life's path instead of making it more tumultuous. I looked in all the wrong places for all the wrong things for a very long time, and then one day I stumbled on someone who brought Yeats's poem to life. I wish I could spare my own daughter my circuitous route to romantic fulfilment. If I could pass on one thing, it would simply be to find a partner who she can imagine quoting these few short lines to her and meaning them.

When You are Old

When you are old and grey and full of sleep,
And nodding by the fire, take down this book,
And slowly read, and dream of the soft look
Your eyes had once, and of their shadows deep;

How many loved your moments of glad grace,
And loved your beauty with love false or true,
But one man loved the pilgrim soul in you,
And loved the sorrows of your changing face;

And bending down beside the glowing bars,
Murmur, a little sadly, how Love fled
And paced upon the mountains overhead
And hid his face amid a crowd of stars.

(1891)

→ ←

Norwegian-born broadcaster and journalist **Mariella Frostrup** spent her childhood in Ireland before moving to the UK at sixteen. In the intervening years she has established herself as one of the leading cultural commentators of her generation, presented programmes for television and radio on a wide range of topics from art to cinema, books to current affairs. She is the host of BBC Radio 4's *Open Book* and has penned her *Observer* agony column for more than a decade.

The Song of Wandering Aengus
W. B. YEATS (1865–1939)
→ ←

CAROL ANN DUFFY

I first read this poem, aged eleven, at school while it was read aloud to the class by our marvellous English teacher, Miss Scriven. It made me cry then and remains my favourite poem now – probably for that reason. I love the sung version of it by Christy Moore and have a painting of it by the textual artist Stephen Raw. Yeats wrote greater poems than this, but this was the word-spell that, for me, filled a gloomy English classroom with light and tears.

JOANNE HARRIS

I was ten years old when I first wept over this poem – too young, perhaps, to understand, but prescient enough to sense its curious echoes of magic and loss. I read it then as a fairy tale; now I read it as something else – a glimpse into a mirror, perhaps, reflecting a possible future. It still makes me cry, not from sadness, but because some things are too beautiful to meet with anything but tears . . .

The Song of Wandering Aengus

I went out to the hazel wood,
Because a fire was in my head,
And cut and peeled a hazel wand,
And hooked a berry to a thread;
And when white moths were on the wing,
And moth-like stars were flickering out,
I dropped the berry in a stream
And caught a little silver trout.

When I had laid it on the floor
I went to blow the fire aflame,
But something rustled on the floor,
And some one called me by my name:
It had become a glimmering girl
With apple blossom in her hair
Who called me by my name and ran
And faded through the brightening air.

Though I am old with wandering
Through hollow lands and hilly lands,
I will find out where she has gone,
And kiss her lips and take her hands;
And walk among long dappled grass,
And pluck till time and times are done
The silver apples of the moon,
The golden apples of the sun.

(1897)

➔ ←

Britain's first female Poet Laureate (2009–), Scottish-born **Carol Ann Duffy** has published more than thirty volumes of poetry including the award-winning *Standing Female Nude* (1985), *Selling Manhattan* (1987), *Rapture* (2005) and *Collected Poems* (2015). She has also written plays and books for children. Professor of Contemporary Poetry at Manchester Metropolitan University, she was appointed DBE in 2015.

→ ←

The nineteen novels by British writer **Joanne Harris** include *Chocolat* (1999), which was turned into an Academy Award-nominated film, *Blackberry Wine* (2000), *Five Quarters of the Orange* (2001) and the Rune series of fantasy novels. She has also published two collections of short stories and co-written two French cookery books.

To a Fat Lady Seen from the Train

FRANCES CORNFORD (1886–1960)

➔ ⬅

JACQUELINE WILSON

I loved this poem when I first read it in my teens. I thought it so searingly sad that the fat white woman was missing out on life. Those gloves imply such a buttoned-up primness. I felt very sorry for this poor woman who will never know love and can't even experience the sensuous joys of nature all around her.

For years while on train journeys I looked out the window for a similar woman in gloves. I imagined her scurrying through the grass, her fists clenched within her gloves, blind to everything but her narrow sense of propriety.

I still love the poem now but I take issue with its pitying tone. Why is the narrator so sure she's interpreting the woman's circumstances? She's merely glimpsed her from a train! Perhaps the fat woman is a hard-working servant on her day off, wearing gloves to hide her red calloused hands? Maybe she's all dressed up in her best clothes to meet a secret sweetheart who appreciates her fat white loveliness. Out of view of the train perhaps she will tear off her gloves and all the rest of her clothes and she and her sweetheart will shiver sweetly in that soft grass.

To a Fat Lady Seen from the Train
O why do you walk through the fields in gloves,
    Missing so much and so much?
O fat white woman whom nobody loves,
    Why do you walk through the fields in gloves,
When the grass is soft as the breast of doves
    And shivering-sweet to the touch?
O why do you walk through the fields in gloves,
    Missing so much and so much?

(1910)

➔ ←

One of Britain's bestselling authors, **Jacqueline Wilson** has written more than 100 books for children, including the Tracy Beaker and Hetty Feather series as well as individual titles such as *The Illustrated Mum* (1999) and *Opal Plumstead* (2014). From 2005–7 she served as Children's Laureate. She has also published three volumes of autobiography. Chancellor of the University of Roehampton, she was appointed DBE in 2007.

Tenebris Interlucentem

JAMES ELROY FLECKER (1884–1915)

→ ←

JAN MORRIS

I first read this little poem in 1958, and it can still bring a tear to my
eyes. It is partly the music of the piece that moves me – the lyrically
simple music of the words – the bird's wistful melody (although I
am told in fact that only male linnets sing . . .) but chiefly it is the
pity of it all. Pity, to my mind, is the most piercing of the emotions,
and the poem is instinct with it. When Flecker died in 1915 he was
only thirty-one and half the world was aflame with tragedy. Perhaps
the compassion that inspired his words was premonitory; the sweet
and gentle hand-clasp of the last line, though, makes my own tears
of happiness.

Tenebris Interlucentem
A linnet who had lost her way
Sang on a blackened bough in Hell,
Till all the ghosts remembered well
The trees, the wind, the golden day.

At last they knew that they had died
When they heard music in that land,
And someone there stole forth a hand
To draw a brother to his side.

(1911)

→ ←

Jan Morris (né James Morris) has published some forty books of travel, history, memoir and fiction. Among the best known are *Coronation Everest* (1958), *Venice* (1960), the *Pax Britannica* trilogy (1973–8), *The Matter of Wales* (1984), *Last Letters from Hav* (1985) *Manhattan 45* (1987), *Trieste and the Meaning of Nowhere* (2001), and *Conundrum* (1974), about her change of sexual role.

Listen!

ELSE LASKER-SCHÜLER (1869–1945)

and

No Solace Here

GOTTFRIED BENN (1886–1956)

➔ ←

CATHERINE MAYER

I remember sitting in a café in Frankfurt trying to read through a smear of tears. I was twenty-two and my first great love had recently proclaimed the end of our relationship. 'I can't imagine life without you,' he told me, 'so I have to try living without you.' In the days that followed I drank coffee while picking through volumes of love poetry for arguments to counter his logic. Instead I came across this dialogue between the German expressionists Else Lasker-Schüler and Gottfried Benn. Their affair has ended. Lasker-Schüler appeals to Benn; she is his soulmate, his wayside. He responds with contempt. Her love is too small a vessel to contain the grandeur of his ambitions. Young and unformed as I was, it was Benn's vision that resonated. I would free my darling and in so doing free myself to explore a world of possibilities greater than mere love.

These poems still bring a tear to my eye, but of regret. I am sorry that so many people – men especially but not exclusively – succumb to the fallacy that propelled Benn to a life of destruction and loneliness. My story is happier. After a break of a few years, my first love and I reunited, eventually parting but remaining close friends. He is the author and poet who translated 'Listen!' and 'No Solace Here' for this book. We each found partners who helped us to understand that being loved is not a constraint but a liberation. From the hills of their hearts we see more clearly.

Listen!
During the night I steal
The roses of your mouth,
That no woman may drink from them.

She who embraces you
Deprives me of the shivers,
I painted round your limbs.

I am your wayside.
Anyone touching you,
Is bound to fall.

Do you feel my very being
Everywhere
Like fine gossamer?

No Solace Here
No one shall be my wayside.
Let your blossoms wilt.
My path flows; is only for me.

Two hands are too small a bowl.
One heart is a hill too small,
To rest on.

You, I forever live on the coast
Beneath the fall of the ocean's blossoms,
Egypt lies before my heart,
Asia is now dawning.

My one arm forever lies in the fire.
Ash is my blood and I am forever sobbing
As I pass the breasts, the bones, the remains
Heading for the Tyrrhenian Isles:

A valley with white poplars in the haze
An Ilisos with meadows for its banks
Eden and Adam and an Earth
Of nihilism and music.

(1913)

TRANSLATIONS BY JEREMY GAINES

→ ←

Catherine Mayer is a journalist and writer who has held staff positions at titles including the *Economist*, the German news weekly *Focus*, and *Time*, where she rose to serve as Europe Editor and Editor at Large. She was president of the Foreign Press Association in London 2003–5. She is the author of *Amortality: The Pleasures and Perils of Living Agelessly* and a bestselling biography of the Prince of Wales, *Charles: The Heart of a King* (2015). The same year she co-founded the UK Women's Equality Party.

Adlestrop

EDWARD THOMAS (1878–1917)

➤ ➤

LYNN BARBER

I'm not sure why this poem moves me so much except that it encapsulates England and makes me feel homesick when I'm abroad. I've never actually visited Adlestrop (and of course it doesn't have a station now) but I know and love that particular type of English countryside – the meadows frothing with willow-herb and meadowsweet at the height of summer, the greenness, the stillness, the blackbird singing. And I love the fact that the poem opens quite banally with an unscheduled stop at a railway station where nothing is happening, but then the eye and ear are drawn to the country beyond till we reach that final ornithological impossibility of hearing all the birds of Oxfordshire and Gloucestershire together. The fact that Edward Thomas was killed soon afterwards in the Great War gives the poem an added poignancy, but I think it would be unforgettable anyway.

KATE ATKINSON

This is my favourite poem and the one that moves me more than any other. In June 1914 the poet Edward Thomas was travelling from Worcester to Oxford when the train he was on made an unscheduled stop – 'The steam hissed. Someone cleared his throat.' Afterwards, Thomas immortalized this fleeting moment.

There are many things to love – the artlessness of the opening line, 'Yes, I remember Adlestrop,' as though we had just joined a conversation that had being going on for a while. The strangely effective use of the word 'unwontedly'. The sense of languid heat conjured up by the 'high cloudlets' and the 'meadowsweet, and haycocks dry'. At the beginning of the poem language is pared down to simplicity – 'No one left and no one came / On the bare platform'. Adlestrop itself is 'only the name'. But then we begin to see a progression, an expansion into something more numinous until we reach the swell of those sublime final lines as the lone blackbird begins to sing and 'round him, mistier, / Farther and farther, all the birds / Of Oxfordshire and Gloucestershire.' This is when the tears come, for the transiency of all things and for the transcendent beauty of these lines.

The moment is made more poignant with hindsight, of course, for this is a lost Eden, on the cusp of Armageddon. Thomas must have sensed that too, I think. He joined the Artists Rifles and was killed at Arras in 1917 without ever seeing his poems published.

Adlestrop
Yes, I remember Adlestrop
The name, because one afternoon
Of heat the express-train drew up there
Unwontedly. It was late June.

The steam hissed. Someone cleared his throat.
No one left and no one came
On the bare platform. What I saw
Was Adlestrop only the name

And willows, willow-herb, and grass,
And meadowsweet, and haycocks dry,
No whit less still and lonely fair
Than the high cloudlets in the sky.

And for that minute a blackbird sang
Close by, and round him, mistier,
Farther and farther, all the birds
Of Oxfordshire and Gloucestershire.

(1914)

➜ ⬅

Known over several decades as Britain's most incisive newspaper interviewer, the English writer and journalist **Lynn Barber** has also published six books including *An Education* (2009), filmed by Lone Scherfig, and a memoir, *A Curious Career* (2014).

➜ ⬅

Kate Atkinson won the 1995 Whitbread Prize for her novel *Behind the Scenes at the Museum* and the Costa Award for Novel of the Year for *Life After Life* (2013) and *A God in Ruins* (2015). She has published seven other novels, including four featuring the detective Jackson Brodie, as well as a play and a collection of short stories, *Not the End of the World* (2002).

The Love Song of
J. Alfred Prufrock

T. S. ELIOT (1888–1965)

➔ ←

BIANCA JAGGER

'The Love Song of J. Alfred Prufrock' is a poem that deeply moves me. It was first published 100 years ago, and is regarded as one of the most significant modern poems ever written. After reading 'Like a patient etherised upon a table', John Berryman wrote, 'With this line, modern poetry begins.'

Trying to understand the meaning of this poem is not an easy task, but the feelings of nostalgia it provokes are unmistakable. To me the poem is about reflections on missed opportunities. The 'overwhelming question' ' "Do I dare?" and, "Do I dare?" ' is a question that haunts me. How many times have we failed to seize the moment because of hesitation?

> And time yet for a hundred indecisions,
> And for a hundred visions and revisions

And looking back would it have been worth while?

And would it have been worth it, after all,
After the cups, the marmalade, the tea,
Among the porcelain, among some talk of you and me,
Would it have been worth while. . .

We will never know.

The Love Song of J. Alfred Prufrock

> *S'io credesse che mia risposta fosse*
> *A persona che mai tornasse al mondo,*
> *Questa fiamma staria senza più scosse.*
> *Ma per ciò che giammai di questo fondo*
> *Non tornò vivo alcun, s'i'odo il vero,*
> *Senza tema d'infamia ti rispondo.*

Let us go then, you and I,
When the evening is spread out against the sky
Like a patient etherised upon a table;
Let us go, through certain half-deserted streets,
The muttering retreats
Of restless nights in one-night cheap hotels
And sawdust restaurants with oyster-shells:
Streets that follow like a tedious argument
Of insidious intent
To lead you to an overwhelming question . . .
Oh, do not ask, 'What is it?'
Let us go and make our visit.

In the room the women come and go
Talking of Michelangelo.

The yellow fog that rubs its back upon the window-
        panes,
The yellow smoke that rubs its muzzle on the window-
        panes,
Licked its tongue into the corners of the evening,
Lingered upon the pools that stand in drains,
Let fall upon its back the soot that falls from chimneys,
Slipped by the terrace, made a sudden leap,
And seeing that it was a soft October night,
Curled once about the house, and fell asleep.

    And indeed there will be time
For the yellow smoke that slides along the street
Rubbing its back upon the window-panes;
There will be time, there will be time
To prepare a face to meet the faces that you meet;
There will be time to murder and create,
And time for all the works and days of hands
That lift and drop a question on your plate;
Time for you and time for me,
And time yet for a hundred indecisions,
And for a hundred visions and revisions,
Before the taking of a toast and tea.

    In the room the women come and go
Talking of Michelangelo.

    And indeed there will be time
To wonder, 'Do I dare?' and, 'Do I dare?'
Time to turn back and descend the stair,
With a bald spot in the middle of my hair –

(They will say: 'How his hair is growing thin!')
My morning coat, my collar mounting firmly to the
     chin,
My necktie rich and modest, but asserted by a simple
     pin –
(They will say: 'But how his arms and legs are thin!')
Do I dare
Disturb the universe?
In a minute there is time
For decisions and revisions which a minute will reverse.

For I have known them all already, known them all –
Have known the evenings, mornings, afternoons,
I have measured out my life with coffee spoons;
I know the voices dying with a dying fall
Beneath the music from a farther room.
     So how should I presume?

And I have known the eyes already, known them all –
The eyes that fix you in a formulated phrase,
And when I am formulated, sprawling on a pin,
When I am pinned and wriggling on the wall,
Then how should I begin
To spit out all the butt-ends of my days and ways?
     And how should I presume?

And I have known the arms already, known them all –
Arms that are braceleted and white and bare
(But in the lamplight, downed with light brown hair!)
Is it perfume from a dress
That makes me so digress?

Arms that lie along a table, or wrap about a shawl.
 And should I then presume?
 And how should I begin?

*

Shall I say, I have gone at dusk through narrow streets
And watched the smoke that rises from the pipes
Of lonely men in shirt-sleeves, leaning out of
 windows? . . .

I should have been a pair of ragged claws
Scuttling across the floors of silent seas.

*

And the afternoon, the evening, sleeps so peacefully!
Smoothed by long fingers,
Asleep . . . tired . . . or it malingers,
Stretched on the floor, here beside you and me.
Should I, after tea and cakes and ices,
Have the strength to force the moment to its crisis?
But though I have wept and fasted, wept and prayed,
Though I have seen my head (grown slightly bald)
 brought in upon a platter,
I am no prophet – and here's no great matter;
I have seen the moment of my greatness flicker,
And I have seen the eternal Footman hold my coat, and
 snicker,
And in short, I was afraid.

And would it have been worth it, after all,
After the cups, the marmalade, the tea,
Among the porcelain, among some talk of you and me,
Would it have been worth while,
To have bitten off the matter with a smile,
To have squeezed the universe into a ball
To roll it towards some overwhelming question,
To say: 'I am Lazarus, come from the dead,
Come back to tell you all, I shall tell you all' –
If one, settling a pillow by her head
        Should say: 'That is not what I meant at all.
        That is not it, at all.'

    And would it have been worth it, after all,
Would it have been worth while,
After the sunsets and the dooryards and the sprinkled
        streets,
After the novels, after the teacups, after the skirts that
        trail along the floor –
And this, and so much more? –
It is impossible to say just what I mean!
But as if a magic lantern threw the nerves in patterns on a
        screen:
Would it have been worth while
If one, settling a pillow or throwing off a shawl,
And turning toward the window, should say:
        'That is not it at all,
        That is not what I meant, at all.'

*

No! I am not Prince Hamlet, nor was meant to be;
Am an attendant lord, one that will do
To swell a progress, start a scene or two,
Advise the prince; no doubt, an easy tool,
Deferential, glad to be of use,
Politic, cautious, and meticulous;
Full of high sentence, but a bit obtuse;
At times, indeed, almost ridiculous –
Almost, at times, the Fool.

I grow old . . . I grow old . . .
I shall wear the bottoms of my trousers rolled.

Shall I part my hair behind? Do I dare to eat a peach?
I shall wear white flannel trousers, and walk upon the
        beach.
I have heard the mermaids singing, each to each.

I do not think that they will sing to me.

I have seen them riding seaward on the waves
Combing the white hair of the waves blown back
When the wind blows the water white and black.

We have lingered in the chambers of the sea
By sea-girls wreathed with seaweed red and brown
Till human voices wake us, and we drown.

(1915)

➜ ⬿

Bianca Jagger is one of the world's leading human rights campaigners, whose many awards include the 2004 Right Livelihood Award, the 1997 Amnesty International USA Media Spotlight Award for Leadership and the 1998 American Civil Liberties Union Award. She is Founder and President of the Bianca Jagger Human Rights Foundation, serves as a Council of Europe Goodwill Ambassador, IUCN Bonn Challenge Ambassador and is patron of Amnesty International's Circle of Conscience.

Papyrus

EZRA POUND (1885–1972)

→ ←

MARY BEARD

I first encountered these four words when I was a student strug-gling to piece together – and make some sense of – the scattered fragments of Sappho, now just small remnants on tattered pieces of papyrus. I wasn't quite sure what to make of Pound's version of one of those fragments. Was it a clever appeal to the power of incom-pleteness and to our fragile connection with the life and literature of the ancient past? Was it a parody? Or was it sending up the futility of so much of classical scholarship? Pound, I half suspected, was asking me to question the point of a life spent working on leftovers like this.

Maybe he was. But the words never left me, remembered – as time went on – as a brilliant and unsettling summary of love, loss, absence and hope: poetry in its rawest essentials. We don't actually need any more than this to guess that spring has passed but may come again, and that Gongula is missed – and may, or may not, return.

And, of course, we each have to fill in those dots for ourselves.

Papyrus
Spring . . . . . .
Too long . . . . . .
Gongula . . . . . .

(1916)

> ←

Professor of Classics at the University of Cambridge, **Mary Beard** has published a dozen books including *The Parthenon* (2002), *Pompeii* (2008), *Laughter in Ancient Rome* (2014) and *SPQR* (2015), and presented such television documentaries as *Pompeii* (2010) and *Caligula* (2013).

Fallen

ALICE CORBIN (1881–1949)

→ ←

MAXINE PEAKE

I discovered this poem, which always moves me to tears, in a collection of women's poetry of the First World War given me by an audience member during my first professional stage production at the Octagon Theatre, Bolton. The play was *Early One Morning* by Les Smith, based on the true story of Jim Smith, a young soldier from Bolton who was shot for desertion during the Great War. I played Lizzie, his girlfriend, whom he met when he was home recovering from being wounded. Lizzie would appear to him during the night as he waited for dawn and the firing squad.

I knew little about the First World War and was so overwhelmed by the horror and death. The way working-class young men were nothing more than cannon fodder. The difference in treatment for deserters with shellshock, depending on which class they were from; officers were sent to recuperate, privates shot and killed.

To me this poem catches the last moments of this young man's life. The beautiful images that surround him while in reality he is in the midst of hell. The memories and elements of nature. That he

imagines his loved one there to comfort him. The idea that their
love has transcended the divide between them, and he finds some
comfort in her bosom in his last moments. It also captures the sense
of loss, and of the young hearts ravaged by this war.

Fallen

He was wounded and he fell in the midst of hoarse shouting.
The tide passed, and the waves came and whispered
     about his ankles.
Far off he heard a cock crow – children laughing,
Rising at dawn to greet the storm of petals
Shaken from apple-boughs; he heard them cry,
And turned again to find the breast of her,
And sank confusèd with a little sigh . . .
Thereafter water running, and a voice
That seemed to stir and flutter through the trenches
And set dead lips to talking . . .

Wreckage was mingled with the storm of petals . . .

He felt her near him, and the weight dropped off –
     Suddenly . . .

(1917)

→ ←

The Lancashire-born actress **Maxine Peake** has appeared in such
TV series as *Dinnerladies*, *Shameless*, *Silk* and *The Village*. Her
many stage roles range from Strindberg's *Miss Julie* to Shake-
speare's *Hamlet* at the Manchester Exchange Theatre, and her
films include *The Theory of Everything* (2014).

Anthem for Doomed Youth

WILFRED OWEN (1893–1918)

➔ ←

EMMA POOLEY

The chaos and sheer noise of combat on the front line are what
stand out for me at the start of this poem. I think it's possible as a
civilian to picture how war looks, especially these days with digital
images from conflict zones. But so hard to imagine the sheer terror
of the sound, and all the threats that every bang or screech implies.
The soldiers' point of view is horrifying: dying like cattle – count-
less, helpless, and often so young. It makes me want to weep with
sadness and frustration at the terrible pointless waste.

The second half of the poem is quieter but even more sad.
Those back home are left with too much time to dwell on their
memories, and mourn. The uncertainty of not knowing how their
loved ones were killed, or even whether they were alive or dead,
must have been a torment. Goodbyes spoken only by teary eyes
indicate the repression of grief, and the lonely desolation of some-
one who has lost their beloved, far away, one of millions killed for
no good reason.

Anthem for Doomed Youth

What passing-bells for these who die as cattle?
Only the monstrous anger of the guns.
        Only the stuttering rifles' rapid rattle
Can patter out their hasty orisons.
No mockeries now for them; no prayers nor bells;
        Nor any voice of mourning save the choirs, –
The shrill, demented choirs of wailing shells;
        And bugles calling for them from sad shires.

What candles may be held to speed them all?
        Not in the hands of boys, but in their eyes
Shall shine the holy glimmers of goodbyes.
        The pallor of girls' brows shall be their pall;
Their flowers the tenderness of patient minds,
And each slow dusk a drawing-down of blinds.

(1917)

→ ←

As a professional cyclist **Emma Pooley** was UCI world time-trial champion in 2010 after winning a silver medal at the 2008 Olympics. She now concentrates on multisport races including triathlon and duathlon, winning the ITU long-distance duathlon world championship in 2014 and 2015.

Suicide in the Trenches

SIEGFRIED SASSOON (1886–1967)

➔ ←

ANNIE LENNOX

This small poem by the English war poet Siegfried Sassoon doesn't so much bring me to tears as it leaves me feeling completely devastated. Written economically without embellishment or sentiment, Sassoon's outrage is delivered as an unapologetic hardcore stomach-punch.

The young soldier boy he writes of represents countless legions of young men who died in the 'hell we'll never know' – of First World War trench warfare. It's informative and poignant to note that 'no one spoke of him again', which is one of the factors that must have prompted this poem.

Sassoon acts in the role of spokesperson for those who had no voice or representation. In the same way, Amnesty International highlights and represents those who are apparently 'invisible' and voiceless. At that point in time it was considered an act of treasonable cowardice to renege on one's duty to fight in combat, and suicide by a soldier was regarded as unspeakably shameful. The term 'post-traumatic stress disorder' wasn't even conceived of until decades later.

Decorated twice, Sassoon impressed many with his bravery in the front line and was treated for shellshock at Craiglockhart Hospital in Scotland, which actually prevented him from being court-marshalled by the authorities.

Suicide in the Trenches

I knew a simple soldier boy
Who grinned at life in empty joy,
Slept soundly through the lonesome dark,
And whistled early with the lark.

In winter trenches, cowed and glum,
With crumps and lice and lack of rum,
He put a bullet through his brain.
No one spoke of him again.

*

You smug-faced crowds with kindling eye
Who cheer when soldier lads march by,
Sneak home and pray you'll never know
The hell where youth and laughter go.

(1917)

➔ ◂

Singer-songwriter **Annie Lennox**'s many awards include eight Brits, four Grammies and an Academy Award. She is also a political and social activist, raising funds and international awareness for such causes as HIV/AIDS as it affects women and children in Africa.

Does It Matter?
SIEGFRIED SASSOON (1886–1967)

➳ ➲

ALLIE ESIRI

I recently came across the story (and I say story as it might be apocryphal) that a young Keats was moved to tears by a particular phrase in Spenser's *The Faerie Queene*. The words that got him were 'the sea-shouldering whale' – conjuring an image so brilliantly that later, as reported by his friend Charles Cowden Clark, Keats would 'dwell in ecstasy' on this phrase. My madeleine moment was not, unsurprisingly, a patch on Keats's. As a young student, bored in a history lesson regurgitating First World War statistics, I came upon this poem by Siegfried Sassoon. It was a direct assault on my naive understanding of war. What Sassoon illuminates, with his simple language and genius satire, floored me and still does.

Does It Matter?
Does it matter? – losing your legs? . . .
For people will always be kind,
And you need not show that you mind
When the others come in after hunting
To gobble their muffins and eggs.

Does it matter? – losing your sight? ...
There's such splendid work for the blind;
And people will always be kind,
As you sit on the terrace remembering
And turning your face to the light.

Do they matter? – those dreams from the pit? ...
You can drink and forget and be glad,
And people won't say that you're mad;
For they'll know you've fought for your country
And no one will worry a bit.

(1917)

→ ←

The British writer **Allie Esiri** is the creator of the apps *iF Poems*, conceived as an educational poetry app for children of all ages, and *The Love Book*. Both anthologies feature acclaimed actors reading poems and are also published in print format. She is also the founder of *Allie Esiri Poetry Corner*, a series of live poetry events.

Strange Meeting

WILFRED OWEN (1893–1918)

→ ←

VANESSA REDGRAVE

'Strange Meeting' is forever accompanied for me by the orchestrations of the composer Benjamin Britten for this poem in *War Requiem*. Only poetry and music can penetrate the strange layer of mishmashed teachings, propaganda and politicians' lies, which encrust the brains of generations, and prevent the cognitive processes which can evaluate, analyse and develop new thinking and engage in new processes. Poems help to keep human beings actually responding as human beings to the sufferings of others. Why are our politicians oblivious to the unnecessary and intolerable hardship of their own citizens, as well as asylum seekers? Poems are a sound antidote to cynicism and solipsism, and . . . murder.

Strange Meeting
It seemed that out of battle I escaped
Down some profound dull tunnel, long since scooped
Through granites which titanic wars had groined.

Yet also there encumbered sleepers groaned,
Too fast in thought or death to be bestirred.
Then, as I probed them, one sprang up, and stared
With piteous recognition in fixed eyes,
Lifting distressful hands, as if to bless.
And by his smile, I knew that sullen hall, –
By his dead smile I knew we stood in Hell.

With a thousand fears that vision's face was grained;
Yet no blood reached there from the upper ground,
And no guns thumped, or down the flues made moan.
'Strange friend,' I said, 'here is no cause to mourn.'
'None,' said that other, 'save the undone years,
The hopelessness. Whatever hope is yours,
Was my life also; I went hunting wild
After the wildest beauty in the world,
Which lies not calm in eyes, or braided hair,
But mocks the steady running of the hour,
And if it grieves, grieves richlier than here.
For by my glee might many men have laughed,
And of my weeping something had been left,
Which must die now. I mean the truth untold,
The pity of war, the pity war distilled.
Now men will go content with what we spoiled.
Or, discontent, boil bloody, and be spilled.
They will be swift with swiftness of the tigress.
None will break ranks, though nations trek from
        progress.
Courage was mine, and I had mystery;
Wisdom was mine, and I had mastery:
To miss the march of this retreating world

Into vain citadels that are not walled.
Then, when much blood had clogged their chariot-
    wheels,
I would go up and wash them from sweet wells,
Even with truths that lie too deep for taint.
I would have poured my spirit without stint
But not through wounds; not on the cess of war.
Foreheads of men have bled where no wounds were.

'I am the enemy you killed, my friend.
I knew you in this dark: for so you frowned
Yesterday through me as you jabbed and killed.
I parried; but my hands were loath and cold.
Let us sleep now. . . .'

(1918)

→ ←

Vanessa Redgrave graduated in speech and drama in 1957. She has performed on stages in France, Italy, Moscow, Tbilisi in Georgia, Buenos Aires, Sydney, Melbourne, New York, Dublin, Edinburgh and London. She has been nominated five times and awarded one Oscar. She loves narrating *Call the Midwife*. She has been a Goodwill Ambassador for UNICEF since 1995. She is a member of Memorial, the Russian human rights group, and also of Amnesty International and Liberty.

Medusa

LOUISE BOGAN (1897–1970)

→ ←

KAREN JOY FOWLER

Someone told me once that all art is about the passage of time and that the passage of time is always about death. So death is always art's subject, either openly so or hidden away. This is what poems, even the celebratory, tell us: Beauty will fade. Happiness will end. Seasons will turn. Death will come.

But this poem in which time does not pass hits me even harder. In my reading, death is still the subject, that particular aspect of death we know as loss. To me, the poem is about those endless days after a death, when each morning begins in the unbearable disappointment of waking up and remembering afresh that someone loved is gone now and always will be.

Medusa
I had come to the house, in a cave of trees,
Facing a sheer sky.
Everything moved, – a bell hung ready to strike,
Sun and reflection wheeled by.

When the bare eyes were before me
And the hissing hair,
Held up at a window, seen through a door.
The stiff bald eyes, the serpents on the forehead
Formed in the air.

This is a dead scene forever now.
Nothing will ever stir.
The end will never brighten it more than this,
Nor the rain blur.

The water will always fall, and will not fall,
And the tipped bell make no sound.
The grass will always be growing for hay
Deep on the ground.

And I shall stand here like a shadow
Under the great balanced day,
My eyes on the yellow dust, that was lifting in the wind,
And does not drift away.

(1923)

➔ ←

The six novels of the American writer **Karen Joy Fowler** include
The Jane Austen Book Club (2004) and *We Are All Completely
Beside Ourselves* (2013). She has also published three collections
of short stories and is co-creator of the annual James Tiptree Jr.
Memorial Award.

Bells for John Whiteside's Daughter

JOHN CROWE RANSOM (1888–1974)

→ ←

A. E. STALLINGS

This poem skirts the sentimental by keeping its precision and distance, and always delivers me to the point of tears.

We never even get the name of the girl, just a patronymic. Spoken in the choral We, the poem evokes her speed and lightness, her quickness, only to take it away, to turn a body into a study. In life, the girl is not quiet or obedient or ladylike (despite being a 'little / Lady') – qualities traditionally valued in little girls – she appears rather to have been a tomboy, 'bruiting' her wars, taking arms against her shadow, harassing the geese with a stick. It is only death that makes her a model child, seen but not heard, serious, prim.

Ransom uses two effective strategies. One is understatement: we are 'astonished' and 'vexed' and 'sternly stopped', death is merely a 'brown study' (a thoughtful mood). The other is that the poem spends most of its time looking away, into the life that was – her larking out-of-doors, the whimsical and lyric description, almost fairy-tale like, of the geese, who cry 'alas' and scuttle 'goose-fashion', before the poem returns to the unbearable.

The short last line of each stanza punctuates the rhymes, emphasizes the lively overflow and spill of enjambment among the middle stanzas, and pulls us up short at the end, where the harsh consonants of 'propped' bang the poem shut like a coffin lid, leaving funereal silence where shouts and laughter were.

Bells for John Whiteside's Daughter

There was such speed in her little body,
And such lightness in her footfall,
It is no wonder her brown study
Astonishes us all.

Her wars were bruited in our high window.
We looked among orchard trees and beyond
Where she took arms against her shadow,
Or harried unto the pond

The lazy geese, like a snow cloud
Dripping their snow on the green grass,
Tricking and stopping, sleepy and proud,
Who cried in goose, Alas,

For the tireless heart within the little
Lady with rod that made them rise
From their noon apple-dreams and scuttle
Goose-fashion under the skies!

But now go the bells, and we are ready,
In one house we are sternly stopped
To say we are vexed at her brown study,
Lying so primly propped.

(1924)

→ ←

The American-born, Athens-resident poet and translator **A. E. Stallings** has published three books of poetry including *Archaic Smile* (1999), winner of the Richard Wilbur Award, and *Olives* (2012), as well as a verse translation of *The Nature of Things* by Lucretius (2007).

I Explain A Few Things

PABLO NERUDA (1904–73)

→ ←

JULIE CHRISTIE

Pablo Neruda is my favourite poet. His work has also brought forth great translations, many of them by the late Robert Pring-Mill, his good friend and authority on his work, who first asked me to read Neruda in translation and to whom I am grateful for my introduction to this hero of Chilean poetry.

When Neruda received the Nobel Prize in 2011 he said that he believed that poetry involved 'equal measures of solitude and solidarity, of feeling and action, of the intimacy of one's own being and the intimacy of mankind, together with the secret revelation of nature'. These are the very ingredients that make me love his poetry.

Born in the deep south of Chile in 1904, he died not long before his seventieth birthday in 1973, in part of cancer and in part, Robert believed, of a broken heart, just twelve days after the death of his close friend, President Salvador Allende, in the coup led by General Pinochet and backed by the United States government. I have chosen 'I Explain A Few Things' (here in the translation

Robert most admired) because it is a great cry of rage against injustice, written during the Spanish civil war but filled with sensuous descriptions of what is being destroyed.

I Explain A Few Things
You will ask: And where are the lilacs?
And the metaphysical blanket of poppies?
And the rain that often struck
your words filling them
with holes and birds?

I am going to tell you all that is happening to me.

I lived in a quarter
of Madrid, with bells,
with clocks, with trees.

From there one could see
the lean face of Spain
like an ocean of leather.

       My house was called
the house of flowers, because it was bursting
everywhere with geraniums: it was
a fine house
with dogs and children.
       Raúl, do you remember?
Do you remember, Rafael?
       Federico, do you remember
under the ground,

do you remember my house with balconies where
June light smothered flowers in your mouth?
                    Brother, brother!
Everything
was great shouting, salty goods,
heaps of throbbing bread,
markets of my Argüelles quarter with its statue
like a pale inkwell among the haddock:
the olive oil reached the ladles,
a deep throbbing
of feet and hands filled the streets,
meters, liters, sharp
essence of life,
                    fish piled up,
pattern of roofs with cold sun on which
the vane grows weary,
frenzied fine ivory of the potatoes,
tomatoes stretching to the sea.

And one morning all was aflame
and one morning the fires
came out of the earth
devouring people,
and from then on fire,
gunpowder from then on,
and from then on blood.

Bandits with airplanes and with Moors,
bandits with rings and duchesses,
bandits with black-robed friars blessing

came through the air to kill children,
and through the streets the blood of the children
ran simply, like children's blood.

Jackals that the jackal would spurn,
stones that the dry thistle would bite spitting,
vipers that vipers would abhor!

Facing you I have seen the blood
of Spain rise up
to drown you in a single wave
of pride and knives!

Treacherous
generals:
look at my dead house,
look at my broken Spain:
but from each dead house comes burning metal
instead of flowers,
but from each hollow of Spain
Spain comes forth,
but from each dead child comes a gun with eyes,
but from each crime are born bullets
that will one day seek out in you
where the heart lies.

You will ask: why does your poetry
not speak to us of sleep, of the leaves,
of the great volcanoes of your native land?

Come and see the blood in the streets,
come and see
the blood in the streets,
come and see the blood
in the streets!

(1936)

TRANSLATION BY DONALD D. WALSH

➜ ➜

Winner of the Academy Award for Best Actress for *Darling* (1965), **Julie Christie** subsequently starred in such films as *Dr Zhivago* (1965), *Fahrenheit 451* (1966), *Far from the Madding Crowd* (1967), *Petulia* (1968), *The Go-Between* (1971), *Don't Look Now* (1973), *Shampoo* (1975) and *Heaven Can Wait* (1978). She has also received further Oscar nominations for *McCabe & Mrs Miller* (1971), *Afterglow* (1997) and *Away From Her* (2006).

Hurt Hawks

ROBINSON JEFFERS (1887–1962)

→ ←

URSULA K. LE GUIN

Robinson Jeffers' 'Hurt Hawks' *always* makes me cry. I've never yet got through the last lines without choking up. Jeffers is an uneven poet, and this is an uneven pair of poems, intemperate and unreasonable. Jeffers casts off humanity too easily. But he was himself a kind of maimed, hurt hawk, and his identification with the birds is true compassion. He builds pain unendurably so that we can know release.

Fearing the weakness tears so humbly, helplessly display, we're proud not to cry. But many of us cry hard at the death of an animal, in life or in books – maybe because the animal's humbleness and helplessness in dying is not ours, or we can pretend it's not ours? Such tears are liberating, and the poet makes them a gift of release into freedom and a fiercer, truer pride.

Hurt Hawks

I

The broken pillar of the wing jags from the clotted
    shoulder,
The wing trails like a banner in defeat,
No more to use the sky forever but live with famine
And pain a few days: cat nor coyote
Will shorten the week of waiting for death, there is game
    without talons.
He stands under the oak-bush and waits
The lame feet of salvation; at night he remembers
    freedom
And flies in a dream, the dawns ruin it.
He is strong and pain is worse to the strong, incapacity is
    worse.
The curs of the day come and torment him
At distance, no one but death the redeemer will humble
    that head,
The intrepid readiness, the terrible eyes.
The wild God of the world is sometimes merciful to those
That ask mercy, not often to the arrogant.
You do not know him, you communal people, or you have
    forgotten him;
Intemperate and savage, the hawk remembers him;
Beautiful and wild, the hawks, and men that are dying,
    remember him.

II

I'd sooner, except the penalties, kill a man than a hawk;
    but the great redtail
Had nothing left but unable misery
From the bones too shattered for mending, the wing that
    trailed under his talons when he moved.
We had fed him for six weeks, I gave him freedom,
He wandered over the foreland hill and returned in the
    evening, asking for death,
Not like a beggar, still eyed with the old
Implacable arrogance. I gave him the lead gift in the
    twilight. What fell was relaxed,
Owl-downy, soft feminine feathers; but what
Soared: the fierce rush: the night-herons by the flooded
    river cried fear at its rising
Before it was quite unsheathed from reality.

(1938)

➤ ⬻

The American writer **Ursula K. Le Guin** has published twenty-one novels (including, notably, the 'Hainish' and 'Earthsea' books), eleven volumes of short stories, five collections of essays, twelve books for children, six volumes of poetry and four of translation. In 2014 she was awarded the National Book Foundation Medal for Distinguished Contribution to American Letters.

Funeral Blues

W. H. AUDEN (1907–73)

➤ ◄

ROSIE BOYCOTT

I've always thought this is one of the greatest poems of love ever written. The penultimate stanza particularly moves me: you are 'my North, my South, my East, my West'. We all want, at least once in our lives, to love someone that much and to be lucky enough to be loved that way in return. I know it is more commonly associated with funerals, but its depth of sadness is possible only because of the depth of love Auden feels.

Funeral Blues
Stop all the clocks, cut off the telephone,
Prevent the dog from barking with a juicy bone,
Silence the pianos and with muffled drum
Bring out the coffin, let the mourners come.

Let aeroplanes circle moaning overhead
Scribbling on the sky the message 'He is Dead'.
Put crepe bows round the white necks of the public doves,
Let the traffic policemen wear black cotton gloves.

He was my North, my South, my East and West,
My working week and my Sunday rest,
My noon, my midnight, my talk, my song;
I thought that love would last forever: I was wrong.

The stars are not wanted now; put out every one,
Pack up the moon and dismantle the sun,
Pour away the ocean and sweep up the wood;
For nothing now can ever come to any good.

(1938)

The first female editor of a British broadsheet newspaper, **Rosie Boycott** has edited *Esquire* (1992–6), the *Independent on Sunday* and the *Independent* (1996–8) and the *Daily Express* (1998–2001). She co-founded the feminist magazine *Spare Rib* (1971) and Virago Press (1973). A regular broadcaster, she has also published five books including *A Nice Girl Like Me* (1984). In 2008 the Mayor of London, Boris Johnson, appointed her chair of London Food.

In Memory of Sigmund Freud

W. H. AUDEN (1907–73)

➤ ◄

SHAMI CHAKRABARTI

Sigmund Freud died in exile in 1939. Auden's tribute, published shortly after, moves me to tears.

During the Second World War, when 'there are so many we shall have to mourn', Freud stood out to Auden. It is the intimate power of the poem that so well conveys the intimate power of Freud, his values and the movement that he inspired. For where would the twentieth or indeed the twenty-first century be without its great revolutionary thinkers, Einstein, Marx and Freud? One sought to understand the physical universe; another, the man-made sphere; and the third, the intimate – 'to think of our life', 'the fauna of the night'.

Yet the beauty of the poem is in the modesty of the eulogy to a great human being:

> . . . in a world he changed
> Simply by looking back with no false regrets;
> All that he did was to remember
> Like the old and be honest like children.

By underplaying Freud's genius, Auden makes his loss more

poignant. By portraying his values and method 'down among the lost people' in contrast with the tyrants everywhere, the poet paints a picture of a man of curiosity and love in a world gone mad.

In Memory of Sigmund Freud
(d. September 1939)

When there are so many we shall have to mourn,
when grief has been made so public, and exposed
        to the critique of a whole epoch
        the frailty of our conscience and anguish,

of whom shall we speak? For every day they die
among us, those who were doing us some good,
        who knew it was never enough but
        hoped to improve a little by living.

Such was this doctor: still at eighty he wished
to think of our life from whose unruliness
        so many plausible young futures
        with threats or flattery ask obedience,

but his wish was denied him: he closed his eyes
upon that last picture, common to us all,
        of problems like relatives gathered
        puzzled and jealous about our dying.

For about him till the very end were still
those he had studied, the fauna of the night,
        and shades that still waited to enter
        the bright circle of his recognition

turned elsewhere with their disappointment as he
was taken away from his life interest
      to go back to the earth in London,
    an important Jew who died in exile.

Only Hate was happy, hoping to augment
his practice now, and his dingy clientele
      who think they can be cured by killing
    and covering the garden with ashes.

They are still alive, but in a world he changed
simply by looking back with no false regrets;
      all he did was to remember
    like the old and be honest like children.

He wasn't clever at all: he merely told
the unhappy Present to recite the Past
      like a poetry lesson till sooner
    or later it faltered at the line where

long ago the accusations had begun,
and suddenly knew by whom it had been judged,
      how rich life had been and how silly,
    and was life-forgiven and more humble,

able to approach the Future as a friend
without a wardrobe of excuses, without
      a set mask of rectitude or an
    embarrassing over-familiar gesture.

No wonder the ancient cultures of conceit
in his technique of unsettlement foresaw
       the fall of princes, the collapse of
     their lucrative patterns of frustration:

if he succeeded, why, the Generalised Life
would become impossible, the monolith
       of State be broken and prevented
     the co-operation of avengers.

Of course they called on God, but he went his way
down among the lost people like Dante, down
       to the stinking fosse where the injured
     lead the ugly life of the rejected,

and showed us what evil is: not, as we thought
deeds that must be punished, but our lack of faith,
       our dishonest mood of denial,
     the concupiscence of the oppressor.

If some traces of the autocratic pose,
the paternal strictness he distrusted, still
       clung to his utterance and features,
     it was a protective coloration

for one who lived among enemies so long:
if often he was wrong and, at times, absurd,
       to us he is no more a person
     now but a whole climate of opinion

under whom we conduct our differing lives:
Like weather he can only hinder or help,
     the proud can still be proud but find it
     a little harder, and the tyrant tries to

make do with him but doesn't care for him much:
he quietly surrounds all our habits of growth
     and extends, till the tired in even
     the remotest miserable duchy

have felt the change in their bones and are cheered,
till the child unlucky in his little State,
     some hearth where freedom is excluded,
     a hive whose honey is fear and worry,

feels calmer now and somehow assured of escape,
while, as they lie in the grass of our neglect,
     so many long-forgotten objects
     revealed by his undiscouraged shining

are returned to us and made precious again;
games we had thought we must drop as we grew up,
     little noises we dared not laugh at,
     faces we made when no one was looking.

But he wishes us more than this. To be free
is often to be lonely. He would unite
     the unequal moieties fractured
     by our own well-meaning sense of justice,

would restore to the larger the wit and will
the smaller possesses but can only use
>   for arid disputes, would give back to
>   the son the mother's richness of feeling:

but he would have us remember most of all
to be enthusiastic over the night,
>   not only for the sense of wonder
>   it alone has to offer, but also

because it needs our love. With large sad eyes
its delectable creatures look up and beg
>   us dumbly to ask them to follow:
>   they are exiles who long for the future

that lies in our power, they too would rejoice
if allowed to serve enlightenment like him,
>   even to bear our cry of 'Judas',
>   as he did and all must bear who serve it.

One rational voice is dumb. Over his grave
the household of Impulse mourns one dearly loved:
>   sad is Eros, builder of cities,
>   and weeping anarchic Aphrodite.

>   (1939)

→ ←

A barrister by training, now a Master of the Bench of Middle Temple,
Shami Chakrabarti was the director of Liberty, the British civil rights
advocacy group, 2003–16. She is Chancellor of the University of Essex
and an Honorary Professor of Law at Manchester University.

Requiem

ANNA AKHMATOVA (1889–1966)

→ ←

ANNE APPLEBAUM

Anna Akhmatova's poem gives voice to the voiceless: the victims of Stalin's mass terror, as well as their mothers, husbands, sisters, sons and daughters. Akhmatova herself was the wife of one victim, the mother of another and the witness of the suffering of countless others. She wrote and rewrote *Requiem* over five years, between 1935 and 1940, but published it only after Stalin's death in 1953. The poem has no hero and no moral, but ends instead with an injunction and a promise: never forget. 'I'd like to name you all by name,' she wrote, 'but the list / has been removed and there is nowhere to look. So, / I have woven you this wide shroud out of the humble words / I overheard you use. Everywhere, forever and always, / I will never forget one single thing.' For many decades, this poem really was the only monument, and the only memorial, that millions of mourners ever expected to have.

Dedication (from *Requiem*)
ANNA AKHMATOVA (1889–1966)
→ ←

KATE ALLEN

When I was fifteen years old I discovered the poetry of Anna Akhmatova. I bought a slim volume of her poetry with a birthday book token and remember to this day reading *Requiem* that first time. Akhmatova's husband died in Stalin's camps. She spent seventeen months in prison queues looking for her son who had been arrested. In the introduction to *Requiem* Akhmatova writes of being in that prison queue in Leningrad when a woman 'with lips blue with cold' asked her 'Can you describe this?' She replied 'I can!' And she could. Her poem is a heartbreaking description of the brutalities of that time mixed with feelings of despair and horror. But the lines my fifteen-year-old self underlined were ones recognizing that hope was still alive:

> For some the wind can freshly blow,
> for some the sunlight fade at ease . . .

She kept that hope alive in the midst of such horror and her *Requiem* is a fitting memorial to the millions who suffered under Stalin. It still makes me cry.

Dedication from *Requiem*
Such grief might make the mountains stoop,
reverse the waters where they flow,

but cannot burst these ponderous bolts
that block us from the prison cells
crowded with mortal woe. . . .
For some the wind can freshly blow,
for some the sunlight fade at ease,
but we, made partners in our dread,
hear but the grating of the keys,
and heavy-booted soldiers' tread.
As if for early mass, we rose
and each day walked the wilderness,
trudging through silent street and square,
to congregate, less live than dead.
The sun declined, the Neva blurred,
and hope sang always from afar.
Whose sentence is decreed ? . . . That moan,
that sudden spurt of woman's tears,
shows one distinguished from the rest,
as if they'd knocked her to the ground
and wrenched the heart out of her breast,
then let her go, reeling, alone.
Where are they now, my nameless friends
from those two years I spent in hell ?
What specters mock them now, amid
the fury of Siberian snows,
or in the blighted circle of the moon?
To them I cry, Hail and Farewell!

(1940)

TRANSLATION BY STANLEY KUNITZ
AND MAX HAYWARD

→ ←

The American-born, now Polish author and journalist **Anne Applebaum** won the 2004 Pulitzer Prize for *Gulag: A History*. She has also published *Between East and West: Across the Borderland of Europe* (1994) and *Iron Curtain: The Crushing of Eastern Europe 1944–1956* (2012).

→ ←

Director of Amnesty International since 2000, **Kate Allen** was Deputy Chief Executive at the Refugee Council running both the Bosnia and Kosovo Emergency Evacuation Programmes. Prior to that she had several roles in local government.

Excerpt from *Four Quartets*: No 4. Little Gidding

T. S. ELIOT (1888–1965)

➜ ⬅

NELL GIFFORD

If you came this way
Taking the route . . .
Is England and nowhere.

I discovered T. S. Eliot as an undergraduate, and this section of 'Little Gidding' described in detail the circumstances of my life at that time. Our family home was being sold and I was heartbroken. It was a dusty rambling old house in a quiet village in North Wiltshire, a country of plain churches, flat waterlogged dairy pastures and overgrown hedges.

This poem exactly describes a return to the village I grew up in, the hedges huge and frothy with May blossom, the rough road, the turn up the drive, the old farm buildings. We lived beside the church and we used to go through a door in our garden wall into the churchyard with my mother every Sunday for evensong. For me, God lived in her devotion, her attachment to the life of that little church, in the quiet evensong, in the peace of that church interior. Yet circumstances had removed my mother from my life and removed me from the life that she had created. By the time I got to university, I was adrift.

But much of the time I was looking backwards to that vanished world, that village, that world's end. I didn't understand why I wanted to go back so much and this poem seemed to be written for me, as an explanation, a set of instructions even. 'You are not here to verify, / Instruct yourself, or inform curiosity / Or carry report.' This was explaining everything to me, and then – 'You are here to kneel / Where prayer has been valid.'

When I read that, I understood that the events and people of the past had been real, had lived real lives, and I felt my life and my past authenticated by that one simple word – valid. And I cried with relief.

No. 4 Little Gidding from *Four Quartets*

<blockquote>

   If you came this way,
Taking the route you would be likely to take
From the place you would be likely to come from,
If you came this way in may time, you would find the
  hedges
White again, in May, with voluptuary sweetness.
It would be the same at the end of the journey,
If you came at night like a broken king,
If you came by day not knowing what you came for,
It would be the same, when you leave the rough road
And turn behind the pig-sty to the dull façade
And the tombstone. And what you thought you came for
Is only a shell, a husk of meaning
From which the purpose breaks only when it is fulfilled

</blockquote>

If at all. Either you had no purpose
Or the purpose is beyond the end you figured
And is altered in fulfilment. There are other places
Which also are the world's end, some at the sea jaws,
Or over a dark lake, in a desert or a city –
But this is the nearest, in place and time,
Now and in England.

　　　　If you came this way,
Taking any route, starting from anywhere,
At any time or at any season,
It would always be the same: you would have to put off
Sense and notion. You are not here to verify,
Instruct yourself, or inform curiosity
Or carry report. You are here to kneel
Where prayer has been valid. And prayer is more
Than an order of words, the conscious occupation
Of the praying mind, or the sound of the voice praying.
And what the dead had no speech for, when living,
They can tell you, being dead: the communication
Of the dead is tongued with fire beyond the language of
　　　the living.
Here, the intersection of the timeless moment
Is England and nowhere. Never and always.

　　　　　　　　　　　　　　　　　　　　(1941)

➔ ←

After studying English Literature at Oxford University, **Nell Gifford** joined Circus Flora in the USA. She would go on to perform with troupes throughout the world, from the Chinese

State Circus to Circus Roncalli in Germany – experiences that were related in her memoir *Josser: The Secret Life of a Circus Girl* (1999). With her husband Toti, she founded Giffords Circus in 2000. It has since entertained over 700,000 people and continues to tour south-west England and London during summer.

The Peasants

ALUN LEWIS (1915–44)

→ ←

ANNE REID

The reason I find this poem so moving is that it's such a simple but vivid, heartbreaking picture of poor, innocent people trying to lead quiet, dignified lives . . . and the wars go on and on. It's a sad picture of the world today.

The Peasants
The dwarf barefooted, chanting
Behind the oxen by the lake,
Stepping lightly and lazily among the thorntrees
Dusky and dazed with sunlight, half awake;

The women breaking stones upon the highway,
Walking erect with burdens on their heads,
One body growing in another body,
Creation touching verminous straw beds.

Across scorched hills and trampled crops
The soldiers straggle by.
History staggers in their wake.
The peasants watch them die.

(1943)

➔ ⬅

The British actress **Anne Reid** has played such television roles as Jean in *Dinnerladies* and Celia in *Last Tango in Halifax*, as well as the title role in the 2003 film *The Mother*, opposite Daniel Craig, for which she received BAFTA and European Film Award nominations as Best Actress.

Excerpt from *The Lost Son*:
5. It was beginning winter

THEODORE ROETHKE (1908–63)

→ ←

FRANCINE PROSE

A student (or maybe by then a former student) sent me Theodore Roethke's beautiful poem, 'The Lost Son', in the late 1980s when my father had just died, and I thought that I would die too – of grief. It's the poem I send now to friends whom I know are suffering. For me the experience of reading the poem feels like the experience of nearly drowning and bobbing up, sputtering, to the surface; or of being critically ill and recovering: of waking up one morning and, as if by some miracle, feeling better. The poem starts in the darkest place one can imagine ('Worm, be with me / This is my hard time') and progresses through more darkness into something like the light, or at least the hope that the 'light within light' exists, and will return. ('A lively understandable spirit / Once entertained you. / It will come again.') I still read those lines over and over, but sparingly. It's almost as if I'm afraid to wear them out. I save them for those times when I most need their beauty, their consolation, their promise.

It is a long poem, divided into five sections; this is the fifth and last.

5. It was beginning winter from *The Lost Son*

It was beginning winter,
An in-between time,
The landscape still partly brown:
The bones of weeds kept swinging in the wind,
Above the blue snow.

It was beginning winter,
The light moved slowly over the frozen field,
Over the dry seed-crowns,
The beautiful surviving bones
Swinging in the wind.

Light traveled over the wide field;
Stayed.
The weeds stopped swinging.
The mind moved, not alone,
Through the clear air, in the silence.

Was it light?
Was it light within?
Was it light within light?
Stillness becoming alive,
Yet still?

A lively understandable spirit
Once entertained you.

It will come again.
Be still.
Wait.

(1948)

➔ ➔

The American writer **Francine Prose** has published eighteen novels, from *Judah the Pious* (1973) to *Lovers at the Chameleon Club, Paris 1932* (2014). *Blue Angel* (2000) was a finalist for the National Book Award. Her other works include three collections of short stories and seven works of non-fiction, including studies of Caravaggio and Anne Frank. She is a Distinguished Visiting Writer at Bard College, and is a former President of PEN American Center.

If You Forget Me

PABLO NERUDA (1904–73)

➔ ⬅

NICOLE FARHI

I was lucky enough to visit Neruda's stunning house in Valparaiso with my husband, David. La Sebastiana more resembles a lighthouse than a regular home. It's all about wood, light, weather and air. Neruda called himself 'an estuary sailor' because he always looked out to sea without going out onto it. Everything about his house is uplifting, just as this poem is. I chose it because it so perfectly expresses what has happened in my own life and what I feel about it: reciprocated love is in a category of experience all of its own. Above all, the poem is not sentimental. It's true.

If You Forget Me
I want you to know
one thing

You know how this is:
if I look
at the crystal moon, at the red branch
of the slow autumn at my window,

if I touch
near the fire
the impalpable ash
or the wrinkled body of the log,
everything carries me to you,
as if everything that exists,
aromas, light, metals,
were little boats that sail
towards those isles of yours that wait for me.

Well, now,
if little by little you stop loving me,
I shall stop loving you little by little.

If suddenly
you forget me
do not look for me,
for I shall already have forgotten you.

If you think it long and mad,
the wind of banners
that passes through my life,
and you decide
to leave me at the shore
of the heart where I have roots,
remember
that on that day,
at that hour,
I shall lift my arms
and my roots will set off
to seek another land.

If You Forget Me   149

But
if each day,
each hour,
you feel that you are destined for me
with implacable sweetness,
if each day a flower
climbs up to your lips to seek me,
ah my love, my own,
in me all that fire is repeated,
in me nothing is extinguished or forgotten,
my love feeds on your love, beloved,
and as long as you live it will be in your arms
without leaving mine.

(1952)

TRANSLATION BY DONALD D. WALSH

→ ←

The French-born fashion designer and sculptor **Nicole Farhi** moved to London in the 1970s to head the design department of French Connection before launching her own high-end label in 1982. She was appointed an honorary CBE in 2007 and has been awarded the Légion d'Honneur.

Timothy Winters

CHARLES CAUSLEY (1917–2003)

➤ ✦

JOAN BAKEWELL

I can see Timothy Winters in my mind's eye: he looks a standard ragamuffin but without the twinkle in his eye to attract adult approval. I can see his poor teachers, too: 'What are we to make of the lad?' they say despondently to each other. But they are too tired and burdened to do much. He irritates them too: not listening, licking his plate. He's hungry, that's why. I start to crack up at the line 'And slowly goes on growing up' – the fate of millions of neglected unloved children making their own way against the odds. Then pomposity steps in: the headmaster saying prayers. But something touches Timothy Winters: he isn't stupid, he isn't lazy, he notices that phrase: 'children less fortunate than ourselves'. He knows them, he feels for them: they could do with some help. And he roars out, 'Amen!' Then this clever and witty poet turns the tables on us and we pray for him: 'Timothy Winters, Lord. / Amen.' I never read it aloud because the tears come every time.

Timothy Winters

Timothy Winters comes to school
With eyes as wide as a football pool,
Ears like bombs and teeth like splinters:
A blitz of a boy is Timothy Winters.

His belly is white, his neck is dark,
And his hair is an exclamation mark.
His clothes are enough to scare a crow
And through his britches the blue winds blow.

When teacher talks he won't hear a word
And he shoots down dead the arithmetic-bird,
He licks the pattern off his plate
And he's not even heard of the Welfare State.

Timothy Winters has bloody feet
And he lives in a house on Suez Street,
He sleeps in a sack on the kitchen floor
And they say there aren't boys like him anymore.

Old Man Winters likes his beer
And his missus ran off with a bombardier,
Grandma sits in the grate with a gin
And Timothy's dosed with an aspirin.

The Welfare Worker lies awake
But the law's as tricky as a ten-foot snake,
So Timothy Winters drinks his cup
And slowly goes on growing up.

At Morning Prayers the Master helves
for children less fortunate than ourselves,
And the loudest response in the room is when
Timothy Winters roars 'Amen!'

So come one angel, come on ten
Timothy Winters says 'Amen
Amen amen amen amen.'
Timothy Winters, Lord.

                    Amen.

                                    (1950s)

→ ←

President of Birkbeck, University of London, **Joan Bakewell** has
been a broadcaster for fifty years, presenting such television pro-
grammes as *Late Night Lineup* and *Heart of the Matter*. She has
also published an autobiography, *The Centre of the Bed* (2003),
and two novels, *All the Nice Girls* (2009) and *She's Leaving Home*
(2011). Appointed 'a voice for older people' by the UK government
in 2008, she was appointed DBE that year and a life peer in 2011.

Sestina

ELIZABETH BISHOP (1911–79)

→ ←

RUTH SCURR

This poem reminds me of my maternal grandmother, who never cried. When my grandfather died after they had been married for more than fifty years, their five daughters cried plenty, but she did not. I spent the night before the funeral with her, drinking tea in her kitchen. The next morning she woke me very early and said, 'Do you think I should cry?' I said, 'If it would help, if you want to, of course.' Then there was an interminable silence while she lay on the bed with me at the end of which she said, 'No, I have already said my goodbyes.'

My grandmother was a voracious reader all her life. I do not know if she read Elizabeth Bishop, but I am sure she would have been moved, if not to tears, still deeply by this poem, especially the last line: 'and the child draws another inscrutable house.' Who is the man with 'buttons like tears' that the child puts into its drawing? Someone who has gone away, for a short time or forever, leaving the grandmother and the child to keep each other company, close together but far apart.

Sestina

September rain falls on the house.
In the failing light, the old grandmother
sits in the kitchen with the child
beside the Little Marvel Stove,
reading the jokes from the almanac,
laughing and talking to hide her tears.

She thinks that her equinoctial tears
and the rain that beats on the roof of the house
were both foretold by the almanac,
but only known to a grandmother.
The iron kettle sings on the stove.
She cuts some bread and says to the child,

It's time for tea now; but the child
is watching the teakettle's small hard tears
dance like mad on the hot black stove,
the way the rain must dance on the house.
Tidying up, the old grandmother
hangs up the clever almanac

on its string. Birdlike, the almanac
hovers half open above the child,
hovers above the old grandmother
and her teacup full of dark brown tears.
She shivers and says she thinks the house
feels chilly, and puts more wood in the stove.

It was to be, says the Marvel Stove.
I know what I know, says the almanac.
With crayons the child draws a rigid house
and a winding pathway. Then the child
puts in a man with buttons like tears
and shows it proudly to the grandmother.

But secretly, while the grandmother
busies herself about the stove,
the little moons fall down like tears
from between the pages of the almanac
into the flower bed the child
has carefully placed in the front of the house.

Time to plant tears, says the almanac.
The grandmother sings to the marvellous stove
and the child draws another inscrutable house.

(1956)

→ ←

Director of Studies in Human, Social and Political Sciences at Gonville and Caius College, Cambridge, where she has been a Fellow since 2006, **Ruth Scurr** is the author of *Fatal Purity: Robespierre and the French Revolution* (2006) and *John Aubrey: My Own Life* (2015).

Of Mere Being

WALLACE STEVENS (1879–1955)

→ ←

REBECCA MILLER

I've known this poem by heart since college. It's about death and
the immortality of language, in part, yet it also opens itself to tran-
scendent interpretation. I find in its cool syllables and the mystery
of its meaning an infinite depth of emotion – something close to
awe.

Of Mere Being
The palm at the end of the mind,
Beyond the last thought, rises
In the bronze decor,

A gold-feathered bird
Sings in the palm, without human meaning,
Without human feeling, a foreign song.

You know then that it is not the reason
That makes us happy or unhappy.
The bird sings. Its feathers shine.

The palm stands on the edge of space.
The wind moves slowly in the branches.
The bird's fire-fangled feathers dangle down.

(1957)

→ ←

Rebecca Miller has written and directed five feature films including *Angela* (1995), *The Ballad of Jack and Rose* (2005) and *Maggie's Plan* (2015). Her films *Personal Velocity* (2002, winner of the Sundance Grand Jury Prize) and *The Private Lives of Pippa Lee* (2009) were both adapted from her own fiction, which also includes the novel *Jacob's Folly* (2013).

Waking in the Blue

ROBERT LOWELL (1917–77)

➜ ⬷

HELEN DUNMORE

This poem stirs great sadness in me. As I read it I think of those I love who have suffered the pain of mental illness. Such suffering is still so often concealed like a dirty secret, or misunderstood. Robert Lowell wrote this poem about his stay in McLean Hospital in 1957–8. It is a witty, gorgeously imagined and desperate vision. Remnants of rhyme hold the poem like stitches which are on the point of coming apart. The hospital's inmates, once stars of the football field or members of elite fraternities are now 'Mayflower screwballs', confined for their own protection. They wallow like seals or whales in the ocean of their anguish. The writing is startlingly beautiful, even alluring, and then comes the bolt of pain that fells the reader: 'We are all old-timers, / Each of us holds a locked razor.' It is almost sixty years since Lowell wrote this poem, but research into mental health has far to go. We read of children with serious mental illnesses who sleep in prison cells because there is nowhere else for them to be secure. We are still waking in the blue.

Waking in the Blue

The night attendant, a B.U. sophomore,
rouses from the mare's-nest of his drowsy head
propped on *The Meaning of Meaning.*
He catwalks down our corridor.
Azure day
makes my agonized blue window bleaker.
Crows maunder on the petrified fairway.
Absence! My hearts grows tense
as though a harpoon were sparring for the kill.
(This is the house for the 'mentally ill.')

What use is my sense of humor?
I grin at Stanley, now sunk in his sixties,
once a Harvard all-American fullback,
(if such were possible!)
still hoarding the build of a boy in his twenties,
as he soaks, a ramrod
with a muscle of a seal
in his long tub,
vaguely urinous from the Victorian plumbing.
A kingly granite profile in a crimson gold-cap,
worn all day, all night,
he thinks only of his figure,
of slimming on sherbert and ginger ale –
more cut off from words than a seal.

This is the way day breaks in Bowditch Hall at McLean's;
the hooded night lights bring out 'Bobbie,'
Porcellian '29,

a replica of Louis XVI
without the wig –
redolent and roly-poly as a sperm whale,
as he swashbuckles about in his birthday suit
and horses at chairs.

These victorious figures of bravado ossified young.

In between the limits of day,
hours and hours go by under the crew haircuts
and slightly too little nonsensical bachelor twinkle
of the Roman Catholic attendants.
(There are no Mayflower
screwballs in the Catholic Church.)

After a hearty New England breakfast,
I weigh two hundred pounds
this morning. Cock of the walk,
I strut in my turtle-necked French sailor's jersey
before the metal shaving mirrors,
and see the shaky future grow familiar
in the pinched, indigenous faces
of these thoroughbred mental cases,
twice my age and half my weight.
We are all old-timers,
each of us holds a locked razor.

                                                    (1957–8)

→ ←

Helen Dunmore is a poet, novelist, short story and children's writer. Her novels include *A Spell of Winter* (1996), awarded the inaugural Orange Prize, *The Siege* (2002) and *The Lie* (2014). She is a Fellow of the Royal Society of Literature and her work is translated into more than thirty languages. Her latest novel is *Exposure* (2016).

Edge

SYLVIA PLATH (1932–63)

➜ ❧

EDNA O'BRIEN

It would be all too easy to conflate the circumstances of Sylvia Plath's life and death with this jewel of a poem. It is true that 'Edge' was written under the sentence of death, yet there is no cry for help, no envisaged consolation and no whiff of triumph. Instead, we have composure, a Parnassian calm, the precise domestic tableau, an indifferent moon and the image of the rose that in lyric poetry ushers in the Beloved, but hers is a rose that bleeds. Make no mistake, a turbulent heart composed these lovely, lofty lines.

I read it again and again and marvel at the unbearable tension, and that within the naked voltage and almost forensic vocabulary there is such restraint and an otherness, confirming this artist's great leap of going beyond the boundaries of self to the created thing. Every word is bevelled, so that the lines, like shards, strike at the deepest core within us. It is this that makes me cry, and the fact that Sylvia Plath left this world so young and with her genius in full spate.

Edge

The woman is perfected.
Her dead

Body wears the smile of accomplishment,
The illusion of a Greek necessity

Flows in the scrolls of her toga,
Her bare

Feet seem to be saying:
We have come so far, it is over.

Each dead child coiled, a white serpent,
One at each little

Pitcher of milk, now empty.
She has folded

Them back into her body as petals
Of a rose close when the garden

Stiffens and odors bleed
From the sweet, deep throats of the night flower.

The moon has nothing to be sad about,
Staring from her hood of bone.

She is used to this sort of thing.
Her blacks crackle and drag.

(1960)

➔ ↩

The award-winning Irish writer **Edna O'Brien** has published eighteen novels, from *The Country Girls* (1960) to *The Little Red Chairs* (2015). Her other works include five plays, eight collections of short stories, two volumes of poetry and four works of non-fiction, including studies of Joyce and Byron, as well as a memoir, *Country Girl* (2012).

Unknown Girl in the Maternity Ward

ANNE SEXTON (1928–74)

→ ←

JACKIE KAY

When I was seventeen, this poem made me cry. I remember: my first year at Stirling University, my tutor Grahame Smith asked us each to pick a poem that we liked and read it to the class. We were then supposed to analyse it. By the time I got to the last lines 'trembling the selves we lose/ Go child, who is my sin and nothing more' I was blubbing. I blurted out: *I just find it so moving* and was unable to say anything more, swallowing fiercely. I was annoyed and embarrassed having made a fool of myself in front of my brand new fellow students, but Grahame Smith seemed sympathetic and not a stranger to the way that poems can provoke tears. 'Unknown Girl' made me think of how difficult it must have been for my birth mother – the mother here, like mine most probably, chooses the only way – survival – in the stormiest of seas ('I am a shore rocking you off') in order that the baby has a chance in life. But it also made me think of belonging – 'bone at my bone' – and of the process of un-belonging that must begin the moment the poem ends, the familiarity that will turn into strangeness; the mother who will become a relative stranger. It was the first poem that I remember reading that was openly about adoption, and that tackled head on secrets and lies, society's labelling of so-called *bastards* and the feeling of the world's disapproval – in this case *all the ward*. She has a keen sense of being watched in the poem, and her own conscience seems to be watching too. Even all these years later, I am still undone by 'Unknown Girl', heartbroken for the mother, for her tender love for her baby, her 'funny kin', for all the mothers in whatever circumstances who lose their babies. It was the first poem that made me realize I could write about adoption.

Unknown Girl in the Maternity Ward

Child, the current of your breath is six days long.
You lie, a small knuckle on my white bed;
lie, fisted like a snail, so small and strong
at my breast. Your lips are animals; you are fed
with love. At first hunger is not wrong.
The nurses nod their caps; you are shepherded
down starch halls with the other unnested throng
in wheeling baskets. You tip like a cup; your head
moving to my touch. You sense the way we belong.
But this is an institution bed.
You will not know me very long.

The doctors are enamel. They want to know
the facts. They guess about the man who left me,
some pendulum soul, going the way men go
and leave you full of child. But our case history
stays blank. All I did was let you grow.
Now we are here for all the ward to see.

They thought I was strange, although
I never spoke a word. I burst empty
of you, letting you learn how the air is so.
The doctors chart the riddle they ask of me
and I turn my head away. I do not know.

Yours is the only face I recognize.
Bone at my bone, you drink my answers in.
Six times a day I prize
your need, the animals of your lips, your skin
growing warm and plump. I see your eyes
lifting their tents. They are blue stones, they begin
to outgrow their moss. You blink in surprise
and I wonder what you can see, my funny kin,
as you trouble my silence. I am a shelter of lies.
Should I learn to speak again, or hopeless in
such sanity will I touch some face I recognize?

Down the hall the baskets start back. My arms
fit you like a sleeve, they hold
catkins of your willows, the wild bee farms
of your nerves, each muscle and fold
of your first days. Your old man's face disarms
the nurses. But the doctors return to scold
me. I speak. It is you my silence harms.
I should have known; I should have told
them something to write down. My voice alarms
my throat. 'Name of father – none.' I hold
you and name you bastard in my arms.

And now that's that. There is nothing more
that I can say or lose.
Others have traded life before
and could not speak. I tighten to refuse
your owling eyes, my fragile visitor.
I touch your cheeks, like flowers. You bruise
against me. We unlearn. I am a shore
rocking you off. You break from me. I choose
your only way, my small inheritor
and hand you off, trembling the selves we lose.
Go child, who is my sin and nothing more.

(1960)

→ ←

The Scottish novelist and poet **Jackie Kay** won the Guardian Fiction Prize for her novel, *Trumpet* (1998), and has published several volumes of poetry as well as her memoir *Red Dust Road* (2010) and her short story collection *Reality, Reality* (2013).

The Bean Eaters

GWENDOLYN BROOKS (1917–2000)

→ ←

NIKKI GIOVANNI

'The Bean Eaters' by Gwendolyn Brooks brings as much happiness to my heart as tears to my eyes. I *know* beans and *knew* Ms Brooks. But mostly I am reminded when we, my mother, father, sister and I, lived in a segregated community, Lincoln Heights, there was an older couple, Mr and Mrs Brown, who lived in a two-room home that I recall was always very neat. My sister and I went to the grocery store, Neal's Grocery Store, on Saturdays for them. Neal was a Korean War Veteran and that was all I can remember about him. We liked going to his store, though. Across the street from us the Greens ran what was called a 'joint'. Music was played all the time. Mr Simmons had, in his garage, a cookie store where you could get two Windmill Cookies for a penny. I still like Windmill Cookies. Mr Renfro, our neighbour in the back, sometime popped popcorn but we were not allowed to trouble him. They were all veterans of one war or another. We, my sister and I, went to Mrs Brown to get her list. We purchased and returned everything to her. We were never allowed to take any money even though a nickel or dime would have been welcomed; Mommy would have destroyed us if we did! Then one day they were not there. I don't remember if we had gone to visit my father's half-brother in Columbus or if Gary and I had gone to see Grandmother in Knoxville. But when we came back they were gone. Mommy only said they were not there any more. Mommy didn't like sad things like death so death was not mentioned. I was grown before I realized they had transitioned to heaven. I still think if there is, indeed, a heaven there are pinto or navy beans at least once a week for all the good folk to enjoy.

The Bean Eaters
They eat beans mostly, this old yellow pair.
Dinner is a casual affair.
Plain chipware on a plain and creaking wood,
Tin flatware.

Two who are Mostly Good.
Two who have lived their day,
But keep on putting on their clothes
And putting things away.

And remembering . . .
Remembering, with twinklings and twinges,
As they lean over the beans in their rented back room that
is full of beads and receipts and dolls and cloths,
tobacco crumbs, vases and fringes.

(1963)

➔ ◄

The African-American writer and activist **Nikki Giovanni** has published twenty volumes of poetry, from *Black Feeling, Black Talk* (1967) to *Chasing Utopia : A Hybrid* (2013). She has also written ten children's books.

Extract from *Let Us Believe in the Beginning of a Cold Season*

FORUGH FARROKHZAD (1935–67)

➤ ◄

SEPIDEH JODEYRI

In 1999 my brother died in a car accident at age twenty-one. I was twenty-three, shocked and couldn't cry at all. All of our relatives wanted to help me cry. But I couldn't drop even a tear, as I couldn't believe the loss of him.

So I decided to help myself cry and started to reread a very sad poem by the most influential Iranian female poet of the twentieth century, Forugh Farrokhzad. And it worked. After reading just a few lines, I started to blubber like a child.

'Let Us Believe in the Beginning of a Cold Season' is the title of the poem, which is considered by some to be one of the best-structured modern poems in Persian. Forugh wrote it when she was in a highly controversial love affair with a married Iranian literary figure and filmmaker, Ebrahim Golestan. Her strong feminine voice in this poem made me cry very hard, while it was reminding me of the truth that she had died in a car accident as well, but at age thirty-two.

From *Let Us Believe in the Beginning of a Cold Season*

And this is me
a lonely woman
on the threshold of a cold season
at the beginning of perceiving a contaminated existence
        of the earth
and the simple and sad despair of the heavens
and the impotence of these concrete hands.

Time passed
Time passed and the clock struck four times
It struck four times
Today is the first day of winter
I know the secrets of the seasons
and understand the words of the moments.
The savior is asleep in the grave
and the dust, the receiving dust
is an indication of quiet.

Time passed and the clock struck four times.

In the street the wind is blowing
In the street the wind is blowing
and I think of the pollination of the flowers
of the buds with thin anemic stems
and this tired, consumptive time
A man is passing by the wet trees
a man, the lines of whose bluish veins
have crept up both sides of his throat

like dead snakes
and in his throbbing temples those sanguine syllables are
        repeated:

- hello
- hello
And I think of the pollination of the flowers.

On the threshold of a cold season,
in the mournful assembly of mirrors
in the dirgeful gathering of pale experiences
in this sunset impregnated with the knowledge of silence
how can one order a person to stop
who travels
so patiently
so gravely
so lost?
How can one tell a man he's not alive, that he's never
        been alive?

In the street the wind is blowing
lonely crows of isolation
circle around the old gardens of indolence
and the ladder,
how low is its height.

They took all the credulity of a heart with them
        to the castle of legends
and now, once more,
how will a person rise once more to dance

and cast the tresses of her childhood
upon the flowing waters
and trample the apple underfoot
that she has finally picked and smelled?

O friend, O most singular friend,
what dark clouds await the day of the party of the sun!

It's as if in the course of an envisioned flight one day that
        bird appeared
It's as if those new leaves that were breathing in the
        passion of the breeze
were verdant lines of imagination.
It's as if the violet flame burning
in the pure mind of the windows
was nothing but the innocent illusion of the lamp.

(1960s)

TRANSLATION BY HASAN JAVADI

AND SUSAN SALLÉE

→ ←

The Iranian poet, translator and journalist **Sepideh Jodeyri** has
published five volumes of poetry, including *An Emptiness is Flow-
ing Under My Skin* (2015) as well as short stories and translations
into Persian of Edgar Allan Poe and the French writer Julie Maroh.

Those Winter Sundays

ROBERT HAYDEN (1913–80)

→ ←

SHARON OLDS

I am honoured to be invited to join in with what in my diary has come to be called Groan Women. I immediately thought of Robert Hayden's 'Those Winter Sundays'.

When the poem begins, 'Sundays too' brings in Saturdays, Fridays, Thursdays, Wednesdays, Tuesdays and Mondays. Without pointing to them, Hayden brings in all days, always – faithful perpetual unsung work. And we feel the cracking of the hands – thirteen 'ck' or 'k' sounds in fourteen lines!

Then as the lines go on, the rich internal rhyme and off-rhyme seem to me to heat up the poem, the harmony making a cosy mesh for us to nestle in. Again, in fourteen lines, there are only six end-rhymes, in an irregular pattern which is part of why the song holds together emotionally while having a fairly informal spoken tone.

To my fellows impassioned by the language of scansion and rhyme scheme I say: abccd! ceff! dbebf! Freedom and music! I would guess this poem might have more rhyme in it than any other in this volume. The poem has ninety-seven words in all. I could not find one word in the poem which does not rhyme with at least one other word in it – and sometimes it is with five or seven or twelve other words or parts of words.

The places I begin to choke up whenever I recite this at a reading are 'with cracked hands that ached', the empathy in that – right away subsumed back into the dazzle of the language (glints and tints as in a bright woods) – 'labor in the weekday weather made' – O lovely wai, and then lovely double spondee (four strong beats in a row, like the ceremonial sounding of a gong) – 'banked fires blaze. No'.

I am moved by 'slowly', the self-knowledge and truthfulness of the speaker of the poem – the luxury, indolence, pamperedness of the slowness, and moved similarly by 'indifferently' – the sullen son or stepson characterizing himself with no sugar. And I'm moved that he gives us some atmosphere, too – fear, and chronic anger, the whole house (humans and temperatures and cracking consonants too) marked by harshness.

But when I get to the next to last line, there's where I weep, at the truth of it – of my ignorance, my lack of gratefulness and mercy, and my lament for those lacks – for the lack of the key word coming in now. Love, what the father was enacting – and it's not fun or easy or pretty. It's labour something like a soldier's or a monk's. The father is as lonely as the son, or more so. And his labour is at least semi-sacred, as well as formal and decreed, part of what a community, a family, can – despite fear and anger and indifference – be founded on.

Those Winter Sundays
Sundays too my father got up early
and put his clothes on in the blueblack cold,
then with cracked hands that ached
from labor in the weekday weather made
banked fires blaze. No one ever thanked him.

I'd wake and hear the cold splintering, breaking.
When the rooms were warm, he'd call,
and slowly I would rise and dress,
fearing the chronic angers of that house,

Speaking indifferently to him,
who had driven out the cold
and polished my good shoes as well.
What did I know, what did I know
of love's austere and lonely offices?

(1966)

→ ←

The twelve collections by poet **Sharon Olds** include *Satan Says* (1980), *The Dead and The Living* (1984), *The Wellspring* (1996) and *Stag's Leap* (2012), which won both the Pulitzer and T. S. Eliot prizes. Olds was New York State Poet Laureate 1998–2000 and is currently a professor at New York University.

Dublinesque

PHILIP LARKIN (1922–85)

→ ←

MAGGIE GEE

Philip Larkin, the 'young' poet of my own youth, has the knack of writing deep things in a conversational voice that suddenly opens into acute clarity. To me this poem will always recall 'one we were fond of', the beautiful scholar and novelist Kitty Mrosovsky, an undergraduate friend of mine who died too young. I like the way Larkin's friendly women dance and sing for their friend despite their 'great sadness', while that 'Kitty, or Katy' makes this a lament for anyone who dies in the flower of their youth.

Dublinesque
Down stucco sidestreets,
Where light is pewter
And afternoon mist
Brings lights on in shops
Above race-guides and rosaries,
A funeral passes.

The hearse is ahead,
But after there follows
A troop of streetwalkers
In wide flowered hats,
Leg-of-mutton sleeves,
And ankle-length dresses.

There is an air of great friendliness,
As if they were honouring
One they were fond of;
Some caper a few steps,
Skirts held skilfully
(Someone claps time),

And of great sadness also.
As they wend away
A voice is heard singing
Of Kitty, or Katy,
As if the name meant once
All love, all beauty.

(1970)

→ ←

The first woman to chair Britain's Royal Society of Literature (2004–8), **Maggie Gee** has published fourteen books, including the novels *Dying, In Other Words* (1981), *The Ice People* (1998), *The Flood* (2004) and *Virginia Woolf in Manhattan* (2014). She has also written a collection of short stories and a memoir, *My Animal Life* (2011). She is Professor of Creative Writing at Bath Spa University.

Walls

OSWALD MBUYISENI MTSHALI (1940–)

→ ←

THOKOZILE MASIPA

The comparison and contrast between manmade walls and the walls of the heart, created by the Creator, are remarkable. Time was, in South Africa – the original home of the poet, Professor Mtshali – when innumerable walls (laws) were created to keep human beings apart and to sow seeds of hatred for those who seemed different from us. Hearts were hardened and atrocities were committed. Simultaneously hearts were protected so that man, who is a great wall builder, would not have the last say. He could not because man was not made on the basis of colour, gender, race or class. It should therefore not have been surprising when, at last, fellow human beings in South Africa ultimately found one another in embrace, when democracy – in terms of our constitution – was ushered in twenty years ago. The spirit breezed through and love simply walked in with ease.

When I reread 'Walls' recently it tugged at my heart and I could not help but cry – with gratitude.

Walls
Man is
a great wall builder –
the Berlin Wall
the Wailing Wall of Jerusalem –
but the wall
most impregnable
has a moat
flowing with fright
around his heart.

A wall without windows
for the spirit
to breeze through

A wall without a door
for love to walk in

(1971)

➤ ➤

Born and raised in Soweto, **Thokozile Masipa** was a social worker
and crime reporter before training as a lawyer, becoming in 1998
only the second black woman to be appointed a Judge of the High
Court of South Africa. In 2014 she presided over the trial of the
Paralympic athlete Oscar Pistorius.

Little Sleep's-Head Sprouting Hair in the Moonlight

GALWAY KINNELL (1927–2014)

→ ←

MICHELLE WILLIAMS

I first met my friend Chris Shinn, the playwright, in a diner that miraculously still exists on the lower east side. We both lived down there then. It was winter and I couldn't figure out how to keep warm. I wore jeans and black high-top Converse, a grey hoodie underneath a jean jacket. I knew a warmer jacket must exist, I saw them on everyone but me, but I didn't know how or where to find one.

We sat at the table deepest in the restaurant, the coziest and most snug spot. They put warm flaky biscuits on the table for free and he, the first real artist I ever met, smiled at me. From my frozen wet feet to my hatless head, I thawed.

We discovered our mutual love of this poem and he said he wanted to meet a partner who had reckoned with and understood the meaning of its last line, 'the wages of dying is love'.

I've been thinking about his words in the years since. It is not a poem about romantic love (the action exists between a father and a child) nor a poem about receiving love (a baby can't give love) but as Chris understood and I've taken all this time to, the best sleeping bag in the world won't keep you as warm as sharing one. I love you, Jonathan.

Little Sleep's-Head Sprouting Hair in the Moonlight

1

You scream, waking from a nightmare.

When I sleepwalk
into your room, and pick you up,
and hold you up in the moonlight, you cling to me
hard,
as if clinging could save us. I think
you think
I will never die, I think I exude
to you the permanence of smoke or stars,
even as
my broken arms heal themselves around you.

2

I have heard you tell
the sun, *don't go down*, I have stood by
as you told the flower, *don't grow old*,
don't die. Little Maud,

I would blow the flame out of your silver cup,
I would suck the rot from your fingernail,
I would brush your sprouting hair of the dying light,
I would scrape the rust off your ivory bones,
I would help death escape through the little ribs of your
    body,

I would alchemize the ashes of your cradle back into wood,
I would let nothing of you go, ever,

until washerwomen
feel the clothes fall asleep in their hands,
and hens scratch their spell across hatchet blades,
and rats walk away from the cultures of the plague,
and iron twists weapons toward the true north,
and grease refuses to slide in the machinery of progress,
and men feel as free on earth as fleas on the bodies of men,
and lovers no longer whisper to the presence beside them
          in the dark, *O corpse-to-be* . . .

And yet perhaps this is the reason you cry,
this the nightmare you wake screaming from:
being forever
in the pre-trembling of a house that falls.

3
In a restaurant once, everyone
quietly eating, you clambered up
on my lap: to all
the mouthfuls rising toward
all the mouths, at the top of your voice
you cried
your one word, *caca! caca! caca!*
and each spoonful
stopped, a moment, in midair, in its withering
steam.

Yes,
you cling because
I, like you, only sooner
than you, will go down
the path of vanished alphabets,
the roadlessness
to the other side of the darkness,

your arms
like the shoes left behind,
like the adjectives in the halting speech
of old men,
which once could call up the lost nouns.

4
And you yourself,
some impossible Tuesday
in the year Two Thousand and Nine, will walk out
among the black stones
of the field, in the rain,

and the stones saying
over their one word, *ci-gît, ci-gît, ci-gît,*

and the raindrops
hitting you on the fontanel
over and over, and you standing there
unable to let them in.

5

If one day it happens
you find yourself with someone you love
in a café at one end
of the Pont Mirabeau, at the zinc bar
where white wine stands in upward opening glasses,

and if you commit then, as we did, the error
of thinking,
one day all this will only be memory,

learn,
as you stand
at this end of the bridge which arcs,
from love, you think, into enduring love,
learn to reach deeper
into the sorrows
to come – to touch
the almost imaginary bones
under the face, to hear under the laughter
the wind crying across the black stones. Kiss
the mouth
which tells you, *here,*
here is the world. This mouth. This laughter. These
     temple bones.

The still undanced cadence of vanishing.

6

In the light the moon
sends back, I can see in your eyes

the hand that waved once
in my father's eyes, a tiny kite
wobbling far up in the twilight of his last look:

and the angel
of all mortal things lets go the string.

7

Back you go, into your crib.

The last blackbird lights up his gold wings: *farewell*.
Your eyes close inside your head,
in sleep. Already
in your dreams the hours begin to sing.

Little sleep's-head sprouting hair in the moonlight,
when I come back
we will go out together,
we will walk out together among
the ten thousand things,
each scratched too late with such knowledge, *the wages
of dying is love*.

(1971)

➔ ◄

The American actress **Michelle Williams** was nominated for Academy Awards for her roles in the films *Brokeback Mountain* (2005), *Blue Valentine* (2010) and *My Week with Marilyn* (2011). Her other screen performances include *The Station Agent* (2003), *I'm Not There* (2007), *Synecdoche, New York* (2008), *Shutter Island* (2010), *Meek's Cutoff* (2011) and *Suite Française* (2015). She made her Broadway debut in 2014 as Sally Bowles in *Cabaret*.

Diving into the Wreck

ADRIENNE RICH (1929–2012)

→ ←

KATE MOSSE

Adrienne Rich was an American poet, feminist and essayist of imagination, sublime elegance of language, and great vision. A dazzling and significant wordsmith of metre, emotion and idea.

An anti-war and Civil Rights activist, a stalwart of the Women's Movement, throughout her life Rich spoke out – and wrote out – against injustice and poverty, against racial oppression, against the belligerent self-interest of governments, against the powerful, against the way women's ambitions were crushed or ignored.

She never faltered.

And she wrote about love and the struggles to be true to one's heart; about the barriers put in the way of love by politics, religion, tradition. A passionate advocate of the rights and responsibilities of the writer, Rich believed poetry should reflect, react, to the world rather than be separate from it.

I first came across the work of Adrienne Rich at university in the early 1980s and her writings have kept me company for much of my adult life since then. Hard to choose one. In the end, I went for the title poem of her 1974 National Book Award-winning collection. Rich accepted the award jointly on behalf of her fellow nominees – and for all women 'whose voices have gone and still go unheard in a patriarchal world'.

That this remains true for so many should bring tears to all of our eyes.

I still have my original copy of *Diving into the Wreck*, yellowing and well-thumbed, the corners turned down and margins filled with scribbled blue notes. It serves as a reminder of how, and why, poetry matters.

Diving into the Wreck
First having read the book of myths,
and loaded the camera,
and checked the edge of the knife-blade,
I put on
the body-armor of black rubber
the absurd flippers
the grave and awkward mask.
I am having to do this
not like Cousteau with his
assiduous team
aboard the sun-flooded schooner
but here alone.

There is a ladder.
The ladder is always there
hanging innocently
close to the side of the schooner.
We know what it is for,
we who have used it.
Otherwise

It's a piece of maritime floss
some sundry equipment.

I go down.
Rung after rung and still
the oxygen immerses me
the blue light
the clear atoms
of our human air.
I go down.
My flippers cripple me,
I crawl like an insect down the ladder
and there is no one
to tell me when the ocean
will begin.

First the air is blue and then
it is bluer and then green and then
black I am blacking out and yet
my mask is powerful
it pumps my blood with power
the sea is another story
the sea is not a question of power
I have to learn alone
to turn my body without force
in the deep element.

And now: it is easy to forget
what I came for
among so many who have always
lived here

swaying their crenellated fans
between the reefs
and besides
you breathe differently down here.

I came to explore the wreck.
The words are purposes.
The words are maps.
I came to see the damage that was done
and the treasures that prevail.
I stroke the beam of my lamp
slowly along the flank
of something more permanent
than fish or weed

the thing I came for:
the wreck and not the story of the wreck
the thing itself and not the myth
the drowned face always staring
toward the sun
the evidence of damage
worn by salt and sway into this threadbare beauty
the ribs of the disaster
curving their assertion
among the tentative haunters.

This is the place.
And I am here, the mermaid whose dark hair
streams black, the merman in his armored body
We circle silently
about the wreck

we dive into the hold.
I am she: I am he

whose drowned face sleeps with open eyes
whose breasts still bear the stress
whose silver, copper, vermeil cargo lies
obscurely inside barrels
half-wedged and left to rot
we are the half-destroyed instruments
that once held to a course
the water-eaten log
the fouled compass

We are, I am, you are
by cowardice or courage
the one who find our way
back to this scene
carrying a knife, a camera
a book of myths
in which
our names do not appear.

(1972)

➔ ⬅

The novels of **Kate Mosse** include *Labyrinth* (2005), *Sepulchre* (2007), *The Winter Ghosts* (2009), *Citadel* (2012) and *The Taxidermist's Daughter* (2014), as well as a collection of short stories, *The Mistletoe Bride & Other Haunting Tales* (2013). She is the co-founder and chair of the Baileys Women's Prize for Fiction (previously the Orange Prize).

One Art

ELIZABETH BISHOP (1911–79)

→ ←

CLAIRE BLOOM

For Elizabeth Bishop, born in 1911, and so contemporary to the great American poets Robert Lowell and Marianne Moore, the art of losing would come to be a familiar way of life. The loss in early childhood of both parents left her to struggle on a lonely path. She was eventually well recognized for her individual and arresting talent. The ironic tone of this poem hides a deep and enduring sorrow, only hinted at in the last, devastating line.

One Art
The art of losing isn't hard to master;
so many things seem filled with the intent
to be lost that their loss is no disaster.

Lose something every day. Accept the fluster
of lost door keys, the hour badly spent.
The art of losing isn't hard to master.

Then practice losing farther, losing faster:
places, and names, and where it was you meant
to travel. None of these will bring disaster.

I lost my mother's watch. And look! my last, or
next-to-last, of three loved houses went.
The art of losing isn't hard to master.

I lost two cities, lovely ones. And, vaster,
some realms I owned, two rivers, a continent.
I miss them, but it wasn't a disaster.

– Even losing you (the joking voice, a gesture
I love) I shan't have lied. It's evident
the art of losing's not too hard to master
though it may look like (*Write* it!) like disaster.

(1976)

→ ←

Cast by Charles Chaplin to star opposite him in *Limelight* (1952),
Claire Bloom has since played numerous leading roles on stage,
screen and television, including Ophelia to Richard Burton's
Hamlet, Lady Anne to Olivier's *Richard III*, Blanche in *A Streetcar
Named Desire*, Nora in *A Doll's House* and Lady Marchmain in
Brideshead Revisited. She has also written two volumes of memoirs.

Verses from My Room

SUSANNA TOMALIN (1958–80)

➤ ✦

CLAIRE TOMALIN

Susanna Tomalin wrote this poem a year before she died. It is a poem of farewell, clearly stating her intention to be gone. It is carefully and beautifully constructed, so that I always read it with pleasure and respect even though it brings tears to my eyes. The picture of the empty room and the person entering it, noticing the shoes piled in the corner, the dropped pen, the photo in the open drawer, the book left open, the coat still wet with rain, is hard to forget. And there is a striking deliberate ambiguity in the last four lines of the poem. The poet's questions to the seeker – the person she heard calling her in the second stanza ('I heard you call me once, so calm and clear') – are real questions spoken by a living voice as she writes them; but at the same time we understand they are questions belonging to a voice that will never be heard again.

The poem has a particular resonance for me because Susanna was my daughter, but I believe it is good enough to speak to others.

Verses from My Room

When you come looking for me I'll be gone.
Time is laid waste where waiting has been done.
Though you might find forever and to spare
And bring it to me, I will not be there.

I heard you call me once, so calm and clear,
As children call each other by their names.
Adults avoid such touching, telling games
And only say what everyone may hear.

Listening is lonely only in the dark;
People and business and the day obscure
Persistent shadows, if they cannot cure
Creases where thought and word have left their mark.

Flatten your nose against the window-pane.
Knock at the door, then open it with care.
You'll find a book left open on a chair,
Thrown on the bed my coat still wet with rain,

Some shoes piled in the corner, and a pen,
Dropped from a pocket, lying on the floor.
Maybe a photo in an open drawer
Will catch your eye, and make you smile, and then

Perhaps you'll speak, although it is absurd
To ask a question of such emptiness,
You'll make your invitation and address
A place as pointless as a voiceless word.

When you come looking I'll be far away.
Will you be puzzled? What, I wonder, say
In your bewilderment? Will you know why
I went and didn't wait to say good-bye?

(1979)

→ ←

Among the ten biographies by the award-winning British writer
Claire Tomalin are *Mary Wollstonecraft* (1974), *Katherine Mansfield* (1987), *The Invisible Woman* (1990), *Mrs Jordan's Profession* (1994), *Jane Austen* (1997), *Samuel Pepys* (2002), *Thomas Hardy* (2006) and *Charles Dickens* (2011). A former literary editor of the *New Statesman* and *The Sunday Times*, she has also published a collection of her reviews, *Several Strangers* (1999).

Sonny's Lettah (Anti-Sus Poem)

LINTON KWESI JOHNSON (1952–)

→ ←

JOSS STONE

Linton Kwesi Johnson is one of my favourite poets of all time – this particular poem always used to make me cry, and still does sometimes.

Sonny's Lettah (Anti-Sus Poem)

> Brixtan Prison,
> Jebb Avenue
> Landan south-west two,
> Inglan

Dear Mama,
Good day.
I hope dat wen
deze few lines reach yu,
they may find yu in di bes af helt.

Mama,
I really dont know how fi tell yu dis,
cause I did mek a salim pramis
fi tek care a likkle Jim
an try mi bes fi look out fi him.

Mama,
I really did try mi bes,
But nondiless
mi sarry fi tell yu seh
poor likkle Jim get arres.

It woz di miggle a di rush howah
wen evrybady jus a hosal an a bosel
fi goh home fi dem evenin showah;
mi an Jim stan-up
waitin pan a bus,
nat cauzin no fus,
wen all af a sudden
a police van pull-up.

Out jump tree policeman,
di hole a dem carryin batan.
Dem waak straight up to mi an Jim.

One a dem hol awn to Jim
seh him tekin him in;
Jim tell him fi let goh a him
far him noh dhu notn
an him naw teef,

nah even a butn.
Jim start to wriggle
di police start to giggle.

Mama,
mek I tell yu whe dem dhu to Jim.
Mama,
mek I tell yu whe dem dhu to him:

dem tump him in him belly
an it turn to jelly
dem lick him pan him back
an him rib get pap
dem lick him pan him hed
but it tuff like led
dem kick him in him seed
and it started to bleed

Mama,
I just coudn stan-up deh
an noh dhu notn:

soh mi jook one in him eye
an him started to cry
mi tump one in him mout
an him started to shout
mi kick one pan him shin
an him started to spin
mi tump him pan him chin
an him drap pan a bin

an crash
an dead.

Mama,
more policman come dung
an beat mi to di grung;
dem charge Jim fi sus,
dem charge mi fi murdah.

Mama,
dont fret,
dont get depres
an doun-hearted.
Be af good courage
till I hear from you.

I remain
your son,
Sonny.

(1979)

➜ ᚷ

The English singer, songwriter and actress **Joss Stone** made her name with her 2003–4 albums, *The Soul Sessions* and *Mind, Body and Soul*. She has since made five more albums, including *Water for Your Soul* (2015) and appeared in TV series such as *The Tudors* (2009–10) and films including *Eragon* (2006).

Grow Old With Me

JOHN LENNON (1940–80)

➔ ←

YOKO ONO

This poem is the last song my husband John Lennon wrote. He wrote it with a golden brush of sunset and I read it through tears without end.

Grow Old With Me
Grow old along with me
The best is yet to be
When our time has come
We will be as one
God bless our love
God bless our love

Grow old along with me
Two branches of one tree
Face the setting sun
When the day is done
God bless our love
God bless our love

Spending our lives together
Man and wife together
World without end
World without end

Grow old along with me
Whatever fate decrees
We will see it through
For our love is true
God bless our love
God bless our love

(1980)

→ ←

Japanese-born, New York-resident **Yoko Ono** is a multimedia
performance artist, singer and peace activist.

Extract from *Ten Cheremiss (Mari) Songs*

ANSELM HOLLO (1934–2013)

➔ ⭠

LYDIA DAVIS

I rarely cry over a poem. Maybe it's easier for me to cry over something that is not so good, something in which the sentiment is very obvious, very frontal, completely lacking in subtlety and finesse. The bluntness of the sentiment may be relaxing, and maybe it is easier to cry when you're relaxed, or when your brain is not asked to be very perceptive. When I read a really good poem that moves me, I am at the same time slightly distracted by how good it is, and by considerations of the ways in which it is good. I am so interested in how it works that my thinking brain is as engaged with it as my heart is. Of course, sometimes my brain is engaged first and then, afterwards, my heart: I am moved simply by how good the poem is. But I would not cry over that – it would make me happy. So, even a sad or very serious poem that was very good might make me deeply happy, or deeply happy at the same time that I am moved, almost to tears.

This very brief poem by Anselm Hollo has both moved and mystified me for the past thirty years or so that I have kept it nearby, sometimes up in front of me on a bulletin board and sometimes only in my memory, though in that case somewhat inaccurately reproduced, even though it is so brief. In the physical form in which I have it, it is printed on a postcard published in 1980 that is worn or damaged by the passage of the decades, two corners chipped away, one edge slightly torn, the front still whitish but fly-specked, the back not yellowed but browned, almost burnt, with age.

Anselm Hollo was born in Finland, and after living in Germany, Austria and England, he finally settled in the US in the late 1960s. He had a long career of writing eccentric, rebellious poems ('give up your ampersands & lowercase 'i's / they still won't like you / the bosses of official verse culture') and translating (from no less than five languages). I do not believe I ever met him in person, but I corresponded with him briefly. I have just reread the one letter I can find from him, and I can tell from it that I wrote him twice about this poem, forgetting, the second time, that I had written him before. The first letter he did not answer, the second he did. He told me then: 'The little poem is a translation from traditional Cheremiss/Mari folk sayings, and I still like it too.'

Several things about the poem mystify me. One is that within such a very short span it inclusively conveys so many contradictory emotions: pathos and humor, absurdity and seriousness, apparently frank and earnest statement and obviously fictive story-telling. Part of the fiction is the narrator him- or herself: who is this 'I'? Surely not the poet. Another part is the knitting of the red wool mittens – surely the poet did not knit them, and surely no one knit them, not even the fictional 'I'. They are a fiction. (I may of course be wrong on all these counts! But then that would be another way in which we have been misled by the poet, teased into believing he is telling a tall tale.)

Then there is the fake monumentality of the project, as conveyed to us: it has taken a lifetime to knit these mittens; they were the project of a lifetime; there was an intention to knit them and it was carried out – though at what cost! The project was monumental, and absurd. But, importantly, the voice of this fictional narrator is not absurd. It is plain, earnest, direct, scared and alone at the end. There is nothing fictional about a life being over. Hollo's own life is in fact over, though long after he translated the poem.

That the life is over is one part of what I find moving, in particular that it is over with just one thing, the poem implies, accomplished – those red wool mittens. One thing, it would seem, that consumed so much attention, that consumed so much of other things, perhaps – time, skill, devotion – that the life itself went by almost unnoticed. The one thing was accomplished, but the life is over. And the one thing was hardly monumental, really, in the end.

What mystifies me is also something I find profoundly satisfying. The question is: how can a three-line poem that is on the surface quite simple and direct – three plain, everyday statements – continue in some way to surprise me, each time I read it, not by its content, which I don't forget, but by something else? I think I may have one possible answer: it may be the change of register within the poem. The opening statement is one that any of us has probably made over and over, in irritation and regret, about one thing or another – that we never should have started whatever it was. The second statement, too, is a familiar one, one we might make about the first, whatever the project was. We are tired, annoyed, impatient with ourselves – it's done now, but we regret it. But the third statement is out of all proportion to what has gone before – huge, devastating, and of a significance entirely different from the first two statements. This disproportion or incongruity is the source of the humor of the last line, but also of its pathos. It is comically disproportionate, but agonizingly true, as though, really, the poet is saying: I never should have started this life, because I have lived it but now it is over.

The poem also continues to surprise me because, try as I may, I never quite understand it.

I find this profoundly satisfying – exemplary – because the poem is doing the rare thing that a good piece of writing strives to do and sometimes manages: it never dies, it never becomes stale and familiar, it perpetually renews itself; it is born and lives over and over; it begins, continues and ends, without losing its freshness and surprise. Smart and capacious though we readers are, this poem somehow evades being learned by us – it defies assimilation.

That is a lot to say about such a brief poem, but it seems to ask for it.

From *Ten Cheremiss (Mari) Songs*
i shouldn't have started these red wool mittens.
they're done now,
but my life is over

(1980)

➔ ◂

Lydia Davis is the author of, among other titles, *The Collected Stories of Lydia Davis* (2009), a translation of Flaubert's *Madame Bovary* (2010), a chapbook entitled *The Cows* (2011) and a poem entitled 'Our Village' in *Two American Scenes* (2013). In 2013, she was awarded the Man Booker International Prize for Fiction, and her most recent collection of stories, *Can't and Won't*, was published in 2014.

The Kaleidoscope

DOUGLAS DUNN (1942–)

➔ ☚

JULIET STEVENSON

This poem, from a collection the poet wrote to his young wife after her death from cancer, often moves me to tears. His loss seems so overwhelming – to him and to us. It is written in a quiet tone, but the restraint of its utterance belies the agonizing rawness of his grief. The steady rhythm of the first eight lines seems to mirror his heavy-hearted ascent of the stairs, where with a glimpse into her room his progress is suspended in a chasm of loss and longing. The practical choices they made in the face of the inevitable – her division of her belongings, his preparing of her meal – seem poignant in the face of what they failed to stave off. And then the poem's rhythm seems to gather steam and spool out as his feelings begin to unravel, and the repeated stress of all those monosyllables – me, my flesh, my soul, my skin – give voice to his collapse into the chasm of his loss. And suddenly the small domestic moment becomes as epic as any threnody from a Greek tragedy. From whom is he seeking forgiveness? From some Divine power? From her, whom he failed to save? From himself? We are left by him and the poem in a state of unresolved unknowing . . . as he is left in a wilderness of her absence.

The Kaleidoscope

To climb these stairs again, bearing a tray,
Might be to find you pillowed with your books,
Your inventories listing gowns and frocks
As if preparing for a holiday.
Or, turning from the landing, I might find
My presence watched through your kaleidoscope,
A symmetry of husbands, each redesigned
In lovely forms of foresight, prayer and hope.
I climb these stairs a dozen times a day
And, by the open door, wait, looking in
At where you died. My hands become a tray
Offering me, my flesh, my soul, my skin.
Grief wrongs us so. I stand, and wait, and cry
For the absurd forgiveness, not knowing why.

(1985)

➔ ⬿

The British actress **Juliet Stevenson** has played leading stage
roles at the National Theatre, the Royal Shakespeare Company,
the Royal Court, and the Almeida, among many others, and most
recently appeared as Winnie in Samuel Beckett's *Happy Days* at
the Young Vic (2015). She won the 1992 Olivier award for her role
as Paulina in *Death and the Maiden*. She appears regularly on Brit-
ish television and her feature films include *Truly, Madly, Deeply*
(1990), *Bend It Like Beckham* (2002), *Mona Lisa Smile* (2003) and
Being Julia (2004). She is a long-standing member of Amnesty,
and for twenty-five years has worked around issues relating to refu-
gees and asylum seekers in the UK.

On Squaw Peak

ROBERT HASS (1941–)

→ ←

KAUI HART HEMMINGS

I love that this poem takes place in such a specific location – on a road to Shirley Lake on Squaw Peak in Lake Tahoe. The speaker, who is walking with a colleague, begins by observing his surroundings, so exquisite that they evoke a feeling 'like hilarity', which gives way to thoughts of his wife's miscarriage, the loss they felt, and his current inability to express this loss to his friend.

This poem leaves me breathless – life is simply unfathomable and amazing. It's vast and tiny, it's abstract and concrete and never cruel, just governed by its own laws. 'You shell a pea, there are three plump seeds and one / that's shriveled.'

I am always fascinated by how the natural world infiltrates our personal narratives, both relieving and compounding our awe and sorrows. It's all inextricable. Beauty, terror, death, love, friendship – '. . . the abundance / the world gives, the more-than-you-bargained-for / surprise of it'.

Hass does it all on Squaw Peak.

On Squaw Peak

I don't even know which sadness
it was came up
in me when we were walking down to Shirley Lake,
the sun gleaming in snowpatches,
the sky so blue it seemed the light's dove
of some Pentecost of blue,
the mimulus, yellow, delicate of petal,
and the pale yellow cinquefoil trembling in the damp
air above the creek, –
and fields of lupine,
that blue blaze of lupine, a swath of paintbrush
sheening it, and so much of it, long meadows
of it gathered out of the mountain air and spilling
down ridge toward the lake it almost looked like
the wind. I think I must have thought
the usual things: that the flowering season
in these high mountain meadows is so brief, that
the feeling, something like hilarity, of sudden
pleasure when you first come across some tough little
          plant
you knew you'd see comes because it seems – I mean
by *it* the larkspur or penstemon curling
and arching the reach of its sexual being
up out of a little crack in granite – to say
that human hunger has a niche up here in the light-
          cathedral
of the dazzle air. I wanted to tell you
that when the ghost-child died, the three-month dreamer
she and I would never know, I kept feeling that
the heaven it went to was like the inside of a store window

on a rainy day from which you watch the blurred forms
passing in the street. Or to tell you, more terrible,
that when she and I walked off the restlessness
of our misery afterward in the Coast Range hills,
we saw come out of the thicket shyly
a pure white doe. I wanted to tell you I knew
it was a freak of beauty like the law of averages
that killed our child and made us know, as you had said,
that things between lovers, even of the longest standing,
can be botched in their bodies, though their wills don't
     fail.
Still later, on the beach, we watched the waves.
No two the same size. No two in the same arch
of rising up and pouring. But it is the same law.
You shell a pea, there are three plump seeds and one
that's shriveled. You shell a bushelful and you begin
to feel the rhythms of the waves at Limantour,
glittering, jagged, that last bright October afternoon.
It killed something in me, I thought, or froze it,
to have to see where beauty comes from. I imagined
for a long time that the baby, since
it would have liked to smell our clothes to know
what a mother and a father would have been,
hovered sometimes in our closet and I half expected
to see it there, half-fish spirit, form of tenderness,
a little dead dreamer with open eyes. That was
private sorrow. I tried not to hate my life,
to fear the frame of things. I knew what two people
couldn't say
on a cold November morning in the fog –
you remember the feel of Berkeley winter mornings –

what they couldn't say to each other
was the white deer not seen. It meant to me
that beauty and terror were intertwined so powerfully
and went so deep that any kind of love
can fail. I didn't say it. I think the mountain startled
my small grief. Maybe there wasn't time.
We may have been sprinting to catch the tram
because we had to teach poetry
in that valley two thousand feet below us.
You were running – Steven's mother, Michael's lover,
mother and lover, grieving of a girl
about to leave for school and die to you a little
(or die into you, or simply turn away) –
and you ran like a gazelle,
in purple underpants, royal purple,
and I laughed out loud. It was the abundance
the world gives, the more-than-you-bargained-for
surprise of it, waves breaking,
the sudden fragrance of the mimulus at creekside
sharpened by the summer dust.
Things bloom up there. They are
for their season alive those bright vanishings
of the air we ran through.

(1989)

> ←

Born in Hawaii, **Kaui Hart Hemmings** has published three novels
and a collection of short stories. Her first novel, *The Descendants*
(2007), was adapted into an Academy Award-winning 2011 film by
Alexander Payne.

Perfection Wasted

JOHN UPDIKE (1932–2009)

→ ←

TINA BROWN

No poem has ever caught so well the personal, quotidian impact of loss as 'Perfection Wasted'. I read it at my mother's funeral and felt as if it had been written just for her.

Its theme is the *complicity* of love, the special way we relate to each of the people we cherish, 'The jokes over the phone. The memories / packed in the rapid-access file.' Note the conversational way it begins, as if we are picking up halfway through his intimate discussion with a friend.

Death interrupts the life-work of building a personality, 'your own brand of magic / which took a whole life to develop and market –'; in small, subtle ways we are different things to different people, 'The slant we adjust to a few,' that helps forge the singular connection.

Updike sees us all as life's players, with our loved ones, as the closest audience, perfectly in synch, 'their response to your performance twinned.' In the last four lines the unbroken flow of one eloquent sentence breaks into staccato phrases, like a clock winding down. 'The whole act. Who will do it again? That's it: no one.'

Just as we have interrupted his thoughts at the beginning, so death interrupts the longing flow of his sentences. It feels, like all great poetry, as if it was written just for this particular moment, with an almost casual, confident ease. It breaks me up, every time.

Perfection Wasted

And another regrettable thing about death
is the ceasing of your own brand of magic,
which took a whole life to develop and market –
the quips, the witticisms, the slant
adjusted to a few, those loved ones nearest
the lip of the stage, their soft faces blanched
in the footlight glow, their laughter close to tears,
their tears confused with their diamond earrings,
their warm pooled breath in and out with your heartbeat,
their response and your performance twinned.
The jokes over the phone. The memories packed
in the rapid-access file. The whole act.
Who will do it again? That's it: no one;
imitators and descendants aren't the same.

(1990)

→ ←

A former editor of *Tatler*, *Vanity Fair*, *The New Yorker* and *Talk* magazines, and founder-editor of the online news magazine *The Daily Beast*, **Tina Brown** now runs Tina Brown Live Media, organizer of the regular Women in the World conferences, and is at work on a memoir, *Media Beast*. Her other books include *Loose Talk* (1979), *Life as a Party* (1983) and a biography of Diana, Princess of Wales, *The Diana Chronicles* (2007).

Clearances

In Memoriam M. K. H., 1911–1984

SEAMUS HEANEY (1939–2013)

→ ←

SARAH WATERS

I'd only read Heaney's poem once, several years ago, but when I was asked to select a poem for this anthology, I knew immediately that this was the one I would choose. I had no idea of its title, couldn't (and still can't) recall the context in which I'd come across it, but I located it online, in a matter of seconds, simply by googling 'Seamus Heaney' and 'potatoes': what had stayed with me, vividly, even while the words themselves had faded, was the image of the narrator and his mother dipping their hands in and out of that saucepan of water, their fingers gently colliding; it was a moment of domestic intimacy that seemed to have come straight out of my own childhood.

I know now that the poem belongs to 'Clearances', a sonnet sequence written by Heaney after his mother's death, and to my surprise I find that when it is read as part of that sequence it feels rather upbeat, a celebration of the amorous intensity – 'all hers', 'Her breath in mine' – that characterises the bond between a child and its parent; the powerful final line is sad, but fond. Read in isolation, however, as I first encountered it, the poem seems quite different to me, and I can discover in that line nothing but a statement of loss – a loss so ordinary and yet so profound that the vividness of memory cannot compensate for it, cannot heal or console it, can only keep it raw.

Clearances
3.

When all the others were away at Mass
I was all hers as we peeled potatoes.
They broke the silence, let fall one by one
Like solder weeping off the soldering iron:
Cold comforts set between us, things to share
Gleaming in a bucket of clean water.
And again let fall. Little pleasant splashes
From each other's work would bring us to our senses.

So while the parish priest at her bedside
Went hammer and tongs at the prayers for the dying
And some were responding and some crying
I remembered her head bent towards my head,
Her breath in mine, our fluent dipping knives –
Never closer the whole rest of our lives.

ZOË HELLER

This poem comes from 'Clearances', a sequence of eight son-
nets that Heaney wrote in memory of his mother. I first read it
twenty-five years ago, shortly after my own mother had died.
It's a distinctly ungushy elegy, which is, for me, a big mark in
its favour. Poems about the dead often have a suspicious whiff
of revisionist history about them; this one, I think, achieves
an exemplary combination of tenderness and honesty. I love
the idea of sheet-folding as a courtly dance of filial tensions.
When I folded sheets with my mother as a child, she always
described the moment when the sheet corners met as 'a kiss'. I
think of that now when I fold sheets with my children, but also
of Heaney's 'x's and 'o's and of 'Coming close again by holding
back'.

Clearances
5.

The cool that came off sheets just off the line
Made me think the damp must still be in them
But when I took my corners of the linen
And pulled against her, first straight down the hem
And then diagonally, then flapped and shook
The fabric like a sail in a cross-wind,
They made a dried-out undulating thwack.
So we'd stretch and fold and end up hand to hand
For a split second as if nothing had happened
For nothing had that had not always happened
Beforehand, day by day, just touch and go,
Coming close again by holding back

In moves where I was x and she was o
Inscribed in sheets she'd sewn from ripped-out flour sacks.

(1990)

→ ←

The novels of the award-winning Welsh-born writer **Sarah Waters** include *Tipping the Velvet* (1998), *Affinity* (1999), *Fingersmith* (2002), *The Night Watch* (2009) and *The Paying Guests* (2014). One of Granta's Twenty Best Young Writers of 2003, she was the same year named Author of the Year at the British Book Awards.

→ ←

The British-born, New York-based journalist and author **Zoë Heller** has published three novels, *Everything You Know* (1999), *Notes on a Scandal* (2003, later an Oscar-nominated film directed by Richard Eyre) and *The Believers* (2008).

Nullipara

SHARON OLDS (1942–)

→ ←

SARAH GAVRON

In Sharon Olds' collection *The Father* she vividly chronicles the details of her father's death and her relationship with him during his illness. I have chosen 'Nullipara', as this particular poem has great resonance for me. The day before my own father died of a sudden heart attack, I was sitting with him in his living room, my feet tucked up on the sofa, when he saw holes in my socks. He immediately offered to get me a pair of his socks to wear. He was a loving father who always had solutions to any problem I faced, big or small – he was, to use a phrase from this collection, 'a safety net'. This poem that describes a similar gesture from Olds' father, moved me greatly.

Nullipara
The last morning of my visit, we sit
in our bathrobes, cronies, we cross and re-cross
our legs. Suddenly he sees a thread
dangling from the cuff of my nightie, he cries out
Stay there! and goes to his desk drawer.

I hold my wrist out to him
and he stares with rigid concentration
his irises balls of impacted matter.
He opens the shears, weighty and silvery-
brassy, the colour of taint, he gets the
blades on either side of the thread
close to the cuff – he wants to get it
exactly right, to do me a service
at the end of his life. He snips once
and we sigh, we get fresh coffee and feel it
enter us. He knows he will live in me
after he is dead, I will carry him like a mother.
I do not know if I will ever deliver.

(1992)

➔ ←

The films directed by **Sarah Gavron** include *This Little Life*
(2003), *Brick Lane* (2007), *Village at the End of the World* (2012)
and *Suffragette* (2015), starring Carey Mulligan, Helena Bonham
Carter and Meryl Streep.

When Death Comes

MARY OLIVER (1935–)

→ ←

HELENA KENNEDY

I know Mary Oliver, the Pulitzer Prize-winning American poet. We met because my family always vacation in Cape Cod, and she used to live there in Provincetown as part of its wonderful arts community. She is a very good poet, now in her eighties. I think this poem is about living a good life and embracing the fact that death is all part of that.

When Death Comes
When death comes
like the hungry bear in autumn;
when death comes and takes all the bright coins from his
     purse

to buy me, and snaps the purse shut;
when death comes
like the measle-pox

when death comes
like an iceberg between the shoulder blades,

I want to step through the door full of curiosity,
        wondering:
what is it going to be like, that cottage of darkness?

And therefore I look upon everything
as a brotherhood and a sisterhood,
and I look upon time as no more than an idea,
and I consider eternity as another possibility,

and I think of each life as a flower, as common
as a field daisy, and as singular,

and each name a comfortable music in the mouth,
tending, as all music does, toward silence,

and each body a lion of courage, and something
precious to the earth.

When it's over, I want to say: all my life
I was a bride married to amazement.
I was the bridegroom, taking the world into my arms.

When it's over, I don't want to wonder
if I have made of my life something particular, and real.

I don't want to find myself sighing and frightened,
or full of argument.

I don't want to end up simply having visited this world.

(1992)

→ ←

Author and broadcaster, barrister and human rights campaigner, **Helena Kennedy** is Principal of Mansfield College, Oxford. Chair of Justice and Patron of Rights Watch (UK), among many other public roles, her books include *Eve Was Framed* (1993) and *Just Law* (2004). She was created a life peer in 1997.

Late Fragment

RAYMOND CARVER (1938–88)

➤ ☜

MIRANDA HART

I am not well versed in poetry (pun absolutely intended) but it is something I am beginning to explore with much excitement. I hope this anthology proves a lovely starting point for others in the same boat.

A friend of mine introduced me to this Raymond Carver poem and although it may not strike you as one that might obviously make someone cry, I can explain why it brings a tear to my eye.

You see, I am passionate about people being free. Free to be themselves. Free to feel whole; to feel loveable; to have a sense of self-worth and purpose in their life. To be free from peer pressure, from comparison, from things they feel they 'should' be doing rather than things that make their distinct hearts skip. I don't see calling oneself beloved as arrogant, I see it as freedom to love others because you can love and accept yourself.

Seeing anyone who doesn't believe in themselves, who is harsh on themselves and can't see the wonderful unique human that they are always makes me cry. I hope and pray that everyone at some stage in their life can say 'I feel beloved' and 'I know and accept myself'. Raymond Carver clearly felt it was the most important thing to get from this life.

Late Fragment
And did you get what
you wanted from this life, even so?
I did.
And what did you want?
To call myself beloved, to feel myself
beloved on the earth.

(1994)

➜ ⬸

The British writer, actress and comedian **Miranda Hart** is best known for her eponymous BBC sitcom, *Miranda* (2009–15). Her numerous other appearances include, on television, the BBC drama series *Call the Midwife* and films such as *Spy* (2015). Her books include the semi-autobiographical *Is it Just Me?* published in 2012 and *The Best of Miranda* (2014) and, in 2015, she completed a sell-out stand-up arena tour – *My, What I Call, Live Show* – culminating at London's O2.

Minority

IMTIAZ DHARKER (1954–)

→ ←

MEERA SYAL

Every time I read this poem I find myself blinking back tears of recognition, it is like listening to my mother or sister or daughter and sharing a feeling beyond language, how it feels to be a stranger, to belong and yet not belong. Imtiaz Dharker also captures how we can all feel outsiders and alone at certain times in our lives, we can all feel the solitude of an immigrant. And how much a moment of understanding and empathy at those times can mean. What I also find very beautiful and moving is how she as a poet and an outsider understands the need to own that sense of displacement by taking it and transforming it into a creative act, into something beautiful and universal like this poem.

Minority
I was born a foreigner.
I carried on from there
to become a foreigner everywhere
I went, even in the place
planted with my relatives,

six-foot tubers sprouting roots,
their fingers and faces pushing up
new shoots of maize and sugar cane.

All kinds of places and groups
of people who have an admirable
history would, almost certainly,
distance themselves from me.

I don't fit,
like a clumsily-translated poem;

like food cooked in milk of coconut
where you expected ghee or cream,
the unexpected aftertaste
of cardamom or neem.

There's always that point where
the language flips
into an unfamiliar taste;
where words tumble over
a cunning tripwire on the tongue;
where the frame slips,
the reception of an image
not quite tuned, ghost-outlined,
that signals, in their midst,
an alien.

And so I scratch, scratch
through the night, at this
growing scab on black on white.

Everyone has the right
to infiltrate a piece of paper.
A page doesn't fight back.
And, who knows, these lines
may scratch their way
into your head –
through all the chatter of community,
family, clattering spoons,
children being fed –
immigrate into your bed,
squat in your home,
and in a corner, eat your bread,

until, one day, you meet
the stranger sidling down your street,
realise you know the face
simplified to bone,
look into its outcast eyes
and recognise it as your own.

(1994)

→ ←

The British actress and writer **Meera Syal** made her name in television's *Goodness, Gracious Me* and *The Kumars at No. 42*. She has since appeared onstage in Shakespeare, among other leading roles, on TV in such series as *Doctor Who* and *Broadchurch*, and written three novels.

Michael's Dream (from *Atlantis*)

MARK DOTY (1953–)

→ ←

ANNE ENRIGHT

Mark Doty's work has been a touchstone for all those who lost friends and lovers to the AIDS epidemic in the eighties and early nineties. AIDS was a huge personal tragedy that was repeated in house after house, town after town, but it was more than a medical crisis, this was an intimate, shame-bound disease, hard to discuss in public: it was hard, above all, to put the love back where it belonged, between those who were dying, or nursing the dying. Poetry was, for many years, the only form up to the task.

I cried one day, listening to Mark Doty on the car radio – I can't remember the date, but I was on my way to visit a grave. And I cried again, by accident, when I read 'Michael's Dream' for a poetry programme in Ireland. This is a poem about dying and loving – no matter what way we go – and in its insistence on the dream, it leaves the disease behind. Still, these names are the names of real people and their deaths are also particular, of their time. The loss is always there, ready to ambush and undo, and Doty's work is always there too, when I need to remember the courage I saw in those terrible days, and how we rose to meet our sorrow.

3. Michael's Dream from *Atlantis*

Michael writes to tell me his dream:
I was helping Randy out of bed,
supporting him on one side
with another friend on the other,

and as we stood him up, he stepped out
of the body I was holding and became
a shining body, brilliant light
held in the form I first knew him in.

This is what I imagine will happen,
the spirit's release. Michael,
when we support our friends,
one of us on either side, our arms

under the man or woman's arms,
what is it we're holding? Vessel,
shadow, hurrying light? All those years
I made love to a man without thinking

how little his body had to do with me;
now, diminished, he's never been so plainly
himself – remote and unguarded,
an otherness I can't know

the first thing about. I said,
You need to drink more water
or you're going to turn into
an old dry leaf. And he said,

Maybe I want to be an old leaf.
In the dream Randy's leaping into
the future, and still here; Michael's holding him
and releasing at once. Just as Steve's

holding Jerry, though he's already gone,
Marie holding John, gone, Maggie holding
her John, gone, Carlos and Darren
holding another Michael, gone,

and I'm holding Wally, who's going.
Where isn't the question,
though we think it is;
we don't even know where the living are,

in this raddled and unraveling 'here'.
What is the body? Rain on a window,
a clear movement over whose gaze?
Husk, leaf, little boat of paper

and wood to mark the speed of the stream?
Randy and Jerry, Michael and Wally
and John: lucky we don't have to know
what something is in order to hold it.

(1995)

→ ←

The Irish writer **Anne Enright** won the Man Booker Prize in 2007 for her novel *The Gathering*. She has published five other novels, from *The Wig My Father Wore* (1995) to *The Green Road* (2015), three collections of short stories and *Making Babies: Stumbling into Motherhood* (2004). In 2015, she was appointed the inaugural National Laureate for Irish Fiction.

Daylight Robbery

PAUL HENRY (1959–)

→ ←

STEPHANIE DALE

I first came across this poem at the Much Wenlock Poetry Festival, when it was read, along with a selection of other brilliant pieces, by its author Paul Henry. It effortlessly captures the most joyous rite of passage, and equally heartbreaking moment, when a dependent child becomes an independent boy.

Daylight Robbery
Silent as cut hair falling
and elevated by cushions
in the barber's rotating chair
this seven-year-old begins to see
a different boy in the mirror,
glances up, suspiciously,
like a painter checking for symmetry.
The scissors round a bend
behind a blushing ear.

And when the crime's done,
when the sun lies in its ashes,
a new child rises
out of the blond, unswept curls,
the suddenly serious chair
that last year was a roundabout.

All the way back to the car
a stranger picks himself out
in a glass-veiled identity parade.

Turning a corner
his hand slips from mine
like a final, forgotten strand
snipped from its lock.

(1996)

→ ←

The playwright **Stephanie Dale** has written some of the UK's largest community events including *The Witches' Promise* for the Birmingham Repertory Theatre (2012) and the *Chester Mystery Plays* (2013). She is currently writing Dorchester's seventh community play for 2018. She has also written Afternoon Dramas for BBC Radio Four and teaches Playwriting at BSA, Birmingham City University.

Epiphany (from *Birthday Letters*)

TED HUGHES (1930–98)

➜ ⬅

SAM TAYLOR-JOHNSON

I was given Ted Hughes's *Birthday Letters* at a very transitional moment in my life.

Two of the pages in the book hadn't been cut so I took a knife and carefully sliced down the fold to open them up.

'Epiphany' was the poem that lay beneath those pages, it felt like a calling to read that poem before any others so I listened, sat down and read.

In my head the journey that poem took me on was very reflective of the time I was experiencing.

When people say a piece of poetry spoke to them or moved them, I understand. This literally took me from one part of my life into my next chapter.

Epiphany
London. The grimy lilac softness
Of an April evening. Me
Walking over Chalk Farm Bridge

On my way to the tube station.
A new father – slightly light-headed
With the lack of sleep and the novelty.
Next, this young fellow coming towards me.

I glanced at him for the first time as I passed him
Because I noticed (I couldn't believe it)
What I'd been ignoring.

Not the bulge of a small animal
Buttoned into the top of his jacket
The way colliers used to wear their whippets –
But its actual face. Eyes reaching out
Trying to catch my eyes – so familiar!
The huge ears, the pinched, urchin expression –
The wild confronting stare, pushed through fear,
Between the jacket lapels.
                 'It's a fox-cub!'
I heard my own surprise as I stopped.
He stopped. 'Where did you get it? What
Are you going to do with it?'
              A fox-cub
On the hump of Chalk Farm Bridge!

'You can have him for a pound.' 'But
Where did you find it? What will you do with it?'
'Oh, somebody'll buy him. Cheap enough
At a pound.' And a grin.
              What I was thinking
Was – what would you think? How would we fit it
Into our crate of space? With the baby?

Epiphany (from Birthday Letters*)*   239

What would you make of its old smell
And its mannerless energy?
And as it grew up and began to enjoy itself
What would we do with an unpredictable,
Powerful, bounding fox?
The long-mouthed, flashing temperament?
That necessary nightly twenty miles
And that vast hunger for everything beyond us?
How would we cope with its cosmic derangements
Whenever we moved?

The little fox peered past me at other folks,
At this one and at that one, then at me.
Good luck was all it needed.
Already past the kittenish
But the eyes still small,
Round, orphaned-looking, woebegone
As if with weeping. Bereft
Of the blue milk, the toys of feather and fur,
The den life's happy dark. And the huge whisper
Of the constellations
Out of which Mother had always returned.
My thoughts felt like big, ignorant hounds
Circling and sniffing around him.
                        Then I walked on
As if out of my own life.
I let that fox-cub go. I tossed it back
Into the future
Of a fox-cub in London and I hurried
Straight on and dived as if escaping

Into the Underground. If I had paid,
If I had paid that pound and turned back
To you, with that armful of fox –

If I had grasped that whatever comes with a fox
Is what tests a marriage and proves it a marriage –
I would not have failed the test. Would you have failed it?
But I failed. Our marriage had failed.

(1998)

→ ←

Originally a sculptor, **Sam Taylor-Johnson** began working in photography, film, and video during the 1990s, winning Most Promising Young Artist at the 1997 Venice Biennale and a Turner Prize nomination in 1998. Her work has since been the focus of exhibitions and retrospectives in major galleries worldwide. Her photography includes the series 'Crying Men' (2004) – for which her subjects included Daniel Craig, Paul Newman and Robin Williams – and 'Second Floor' (2014), in which thirty-four images captured the private apartment of Coco Chanel (accompanied by a solo exhibition at the Saatchi Gallery). Her work as a film director includes *Nowhere Boy* (2009), about John Lennon, and *Fifty Shades of Grey* (2015), the release of which marked the biggest box office opening in history for a female director.

I Am Selling My Daughter for 100 Won

JANG JIN-SUNG (1971–)

➔ ✦

HYEONSEO LEE

In North Korea, poetry is not given priority on our school syllabus. Instead, we learn and have to memorize national anthems and other songs that praise the Kim dynasty. So when I read poetry now, after having escaped North Korea when I was seventeen, and after having learned to speak English, I liken poetry to song lyrics – musical, powerful, moving and evocative.

Every time I read this poem, by my friend and fellow defector Jang Jin-sung, I see the woman I gave money to when I was a young girl myself, not really understanding why she was sitting, still and nearly lifeless, on the pavement with a young baby in her arms.

Every time I read this poem I think of how many people in my country have died of starvation, of how lucky I was to escape, and to then be able to rescue my mother and brother ten years later, guiding them to safety in South Korea.

Now, it is my mother who cries, every day, for the family she has left behind.

I Am Selling My Daughter for 100 Won
She was desolate.
'I Am Selling My Daughter for 100 Won.'
With that placard on her neck
with her daughter by her side
the woman standing in the market place –
she was mute.
People looked at the daughter being sold
and the mother who was selling.
The people cast their curses at them
but keeping her eyes downcast
she was tearless.
Even when the daughter
wrapped herself
in her mother's skirt
shouting, screaming
that her mother was dying
the woman kept her lips
tight and trembled –
she did not know how to be grateful.
'I'm not buying the daughter
I want to buy her motherly love.'
That soldier came by
with a 100 won note in his hand.
The woman who ran off with the money,
she was a mother.
With the money
she got for her daughter
she bought a loaf of bread
and put a chunk of bread

in her daughter's mouth
as they said goodbye.
'Forgive me,' she cried.
She was desolate.

(1999)

TRANSLATION BY SHIRLEY LEE

→ ←

After fleeing North Korea in 1997, **Hyeonseo Lee** spent ten years hiding her identity in China before finally escaping to South Korea. She is now a sought-after speaker, who travels around the world as an activist specializing in human rights and refugee issues. Her memoir, *The Girl with Seven Names*, was published in 2015.

Extracts from *Battalion 101*

MICHEAL O'SIADHAIL (1947–)

➔ ❖

MALA TRIBICH

In 2012 I was invited to be the keynote speaker on the Holocaust Memorial Day programme in Northern Ireland. Another on the platform was the celebrated Irish poet Micheal O'Siadhail, who read from his collection of poems on the Holocaust, *The Gossamer Wall*. Afterwards he presented me with a copy of the book, and when I started to read it I was struck by his obviously detailed knowledge of the events he was describing, names, dates and places; even the mention of a fellow survivor, my good friend the distinguished cellist Anita Lasker-Wallfisch. When I commented about this Micheal explained that he had studied the history of the Holocaust for five years before starting to write. I found this remarkable, and very moving.

I have chosen the first and excerpts from the second of a series of eight poems called 'Battalion 101' from *The Gossamer Wall* which describes the progressive brutalization of the members of a Unit called the Reserve Police Battalion 101, which was the subject of a book by the American historian Christopher Browning, called

Ordinary Men. The Unit was under the command of the SS Police Leader Odilo Globocnik, who had been charged personally by Heinrich Himmler with the extermination of all the Jews in central Poland.

In mid-December 1942, in the ghetto in my home town, Piotrków, my mother and younger sister were among some 600 women, children and elderly men who were rounded up and imprisoned in the desecrated great synagogue for a week without water, warmth, food or hygienic facilities. At dawn on Sunday 20th they were marched in groups of fifty to the nearby Rakow forest, made to undress facing newly dug trenches in which they were to be buried, and shot. Only my mother's quick thinking saved me from being among them.

This is why these poems make me cry.

From *Battalion 101*
Point-blank

Blueprint for a cleansed Europe. *Judenfrei*.
March '42 to February '43
at least three quarters of all the butchery.

Timetablers, a retinue of paper Rommels
shunt millions until there's only a residue,
a last few rump-ghettos and labour camps.

Feats of planning. Meticulous follow through.
But who rounded them up in scattered villages
sealed the trains or slew the lame and frail?

Everyday men. The plain and run-of-the-mill
as Battalion 101 whose rank and file
would shy at first from point-blank slaughter.

Truckers, stevedores from Hamburg's docklands,
waiters, factory hands, clerks and small-time
salesmen; an average trawl of average citizens.

A mean of thirty-nine, too old for soldiers,
but drafted as *Ordnungspolizei* to clean up
Poland between the River Wisla and the Bug.

Men long grown before the black sun shone
from a city well-known for ease with outsiders.
Peer conformity, some bone-bred deference

Or any war's need to annul the victim's face?
Humdrum murder, dull and commonplace
as weeks lull them into a norm of violence.

Resettlements. Proceed as usual. Smoothly
again without incidents. Immunities of routine.
Ordinary men hardening in their daily carnage.

Excerpts from A Polish Village
4 Lesson

Company platoons surround the village.
Fugitives are shot. The others round
them up in the market. Anyone gives
trouble, gun them with infants or feeble

or any who hide. Able-bodied men
set aside for camps as 'work Jews'.
The rest shuttled from the market place
to a nearby forest and the firing squads.
A swift session in how best to kill.
The battalion doctor (a gifted piano
accordionist at soirées) in order to show
the ways you ensure an instant release
depicts the contour of a human head
and shoulders, shows a fixed bayonet
set on the backbone above the blades.
Freighted forty at a time to the woods,
victims climb down to be assigned
a policeman each, lined up and pressed
to sites in the forest Wohlauf chose
and made now to lie in rows, a bayonet
as prescribed above each shoulder blade.
The sound of a first fusillade. Work-Jews
Throw themselves on the ground and weep.

Excerpt from *5 Haste*

Wohlauf all day keeps on the go
choosing sites so the incoming batch
won't see corpses. Two squads despatch
truckloads in relays. A messy business.
A blundered aim and blood sprays
anywhere. Splinters of sundered skulls.
The flurried officers begin to despair.
Men from the market are brought in.
Everyone ought to shoot. Hurried

changes to the process: a two-man escort
to the sites for speed. A few who ask
are sent to different task, but Wohlauf
refuses his men any other assignment:
'If you can't take it, then lie down
with all the Jews.'

(2002)

→ ←

A survivor of the Piotrków ghetto and the Ravensbrück and
Bergen-Belsen concentration camps, Polish-born **Mala Tribich**
(née Mala Helfgott) has lived in England since 1947. Her wartime
testimony can be found in the book *Survival: Holocaust Survivors
Tell Their Story.*

The Last Part

DEBORAH KEILY

→ ←

OLIVIA COLMAN

Deborah Keily wrote this poem shortly before her death from breast cancer in 2004. It was read at her funeral and later used in a beautiful, very powerful BBC radio drama called *Goodbye*, by Deborah's friend Morwenna Banks, in which I played alongside Natascha McElhone. I haven't once been able to read it without crying.

The Last Part
They say 'I don't know how you do it.
No-one can do it like you.'
I've made this part my own.
This is not the role I would have chosen, you know
I could be the supportive friend
Not the falling star.
I'd rather be up there – draped in Issey Miyake
Or perfectly belted in Prada –
Than down here boxed, never to be unwrapped.

But – fill in the cliché as appropriate –
God never sends us anything we cannot cope with.
What doesn't kill you makes you stronger.
Of course, it could do both
In either order.

I count my blessings. I am lucky and skilful.
Happiness glistens in my life like jewels under lights.
I have a talent for finding, seizing, holding onto joy.
Friends and family are too small, as words, for this
      perfect harvest.

The parting is bitter though.
Sometimes, in the darkest hours, pre-dawn
I hear taxi engines churning
Maybe a limo to the airport, such as used to come for me.
And I think it's time
For me to head to a more unknown destination
Slim again, furred and painted
I will slip into the back
And catch the driver's eye.
'What time do we need to be there?' he says.
Any time now, I say.
Any time now.

(2004)

→ ←

A triple BAFTA award-winner, **Olivia Colman** has starred in such television series as *Peep Show*, *Green Wing*, *Beautiful People*, *Rev* and *Broadchurch*. Her films include *Tyrannosaur* (2011), *The Iron Lady* (2011), *Hyde Park on Hudson* (2012), *London Road* (2015) and *The Lobster* (2015).

Our Neighbours

FELIX DENNIS (1947–2014)

➤ ⤙

JOANNA LUMLEY

I came to Felix Dennis's poetry only very recently: and it was rather marvellous to know that he only started writing his poetry in earnest as the shadows began to lengthen in his own life. He writes with a complete and God-given talent, to my mind. The words seem to tumble and fall onto the pages straight out of his head, and the easy way they read belies their really wonderful and wise content. He writes like an artist, and loves life in the way only very lucky survivors can.

In this poem, he addresses a theme close to my own heart which is the way mankind treats all other creatures, the 'neighbours' of the title. Bound up as I am in as many animal charities as I can manage, his words are a revelation; 'They bear no judas gifts to blight the land' and 'They dig no graves, nor mines. They scar no hills.' Tree-huggers (me) love the terrible list he reels off of the human hubris and indifference compared with the clean and straightforward way all other creatures behave.

Our Neighbours

'Of fur and feather, scale and shell,
Those neighbours we consign to hell . . .'

They use no jails, except those built by men,
     No management, no coin, no entourage;
They rest content, while we must stalk the world,
     Our so-called sentience, mere camouflage.
We lack their speed, their balance and their sight;
     The skill of merely being what we are
Has long been lost to us. But not to them!
     They make community, but pass no jar
Among themselves to drown the gods of wrath.
     They do no ill, far less do they conspire
To pox the world with gulags – or with slaves;
     Not one has ever sought a man for hire.

They foul no earth, they scorch no forest black;
     And if they kill, they feed upon the lame.
They scourge no lakes, nor fill the sea with wrack.
     They mate beneath the sun and not in shame;
They bind the world – mysterious, in such ways
     As we have yet to learn or understand.
They dig no graves, nor mines. They scar no hills.
     They bear no judas gifts to blight the land.
They know no guilt – nor have they reason to –
     If courtesy could salvage men's despite,
Have they not paid due ransom? Search your heart:
     Their beauty is a child's chief delight.

(2004)

➔ ➔

The actress and writer **Joanna Lumley** has starred in *The New Avengers* and *Absolutely Fabulous* as well as making several television travel documentaries. Her films range from *On Her Majesty's Secret Service* (1969) to *The Wolf of Wall Street* (2013). Among her books are three volumes of memoirs, including *No Room for Secrets* (2004) and *Absolutely* (2011). She is also known for her campaigning social work, on behalf of animals, the Gurkhas and many other causes.

Revenge

TAHA MUHAMMAD ALI (1931–2011)

→ ←

RUTH OZEKI

When I visited Israel and Palestine in 2009, I got a brief glimpse of the geological and narrative complexity of this ancient region. Every rock and stone is filled with stories, and to overturn a stone is to engage with history. Here, point of view is everything, and every stone has many facets.

With his poetry, Taha Muhammad Ali overturned stones. A Palestinian poet, he was born in 1931 in a small village in the Galilee, which was bulldozed during the 1948 War to make room for an Israeli settlement. Later, he lived in Nazareth, where he operated a souvenir stand at the Church of the Annunciation, selling postcards, menorahs and Virgin Mary busts to tourists. He never made it past fourth grade, but he knew he wanted to write poetry. He read Steinbeck, Shakespeare, the English Romantics and classical Arabic verse. He wrote his first poem at forty, and over the years his little shop – the Prominent Souvenir Center of Nazareth – became a kind of informal literary salon.

The grief he evokes in 'Revenge' is ancient yet familiar. A father has been killed, a village razed. The poet starts to rehearse his revenge, but before his enemy can appear, he begins to transform him as only a poet can, word-by-word, line-by-line, stanza-by-stanza. As he shares with his enemy his own most precious and intimate familial bonds, the poem becomes a heroic performance of the effort of imagination required to convince ourselves to overturn stones instead of hurling them.

'In my poetry,' Taha Muhammad Ali said in an interview, 'there is no Palestine, no Israel. But, in my poetry, suffering, sadness, longing, fear, together, make the results: Palestine and Israel. The art is to take from life something real, then to build it anew with your imagination.' He died in 2011, at the age of eighty.

Revenge
At times . . . I wish
I could meet in a duel
the man who killed my father
and razed our home,
expelling me
into
a narrow country.
And if he killed me,
I'd rest at last,
and if I were ready –
I would take my revenge!

*

But if it came to light,
when my rival appeared,
that he had a mother
waiting for him,

or a father who'd put
his right hand over
the heart's place in his chest
whenever his son was late
even by just a quarter-hour
for a meeting they'd set –
then I would not kill him,
even if I could.

*

Likewise . . . I
would not murder him
if it were soon made clear
that he had a brother or sisters
who loved him and constantly longed to see him.
Or if he had a wife to greet him
and children who
couldn't bear his absence
and whom his gifts would thrill.
Or if he had
friends or companions,
neighbors he knew
or allies from prison
or a hospital room,
or classmates from his school . . .
asking about him
and sending him regards.

*

But if he turned
out to be on his own –
cut off like a branch from a tree –
without a mother or father,
with neither a brother nor sister,
wifeless, without a child,
and without kin or neighbors or friends,
colleagues or companions,
then I'd add not a thing to his pain
within that aloneness –
not the torment of death,
and not the sorrow of passing away.
Instead I'd be content
to ignore him when I passed him by
on the street – as I
convinced myself
that paying him no attention
in itself was a kind of revenge.

(2006)

TRANSLATION BY PETER COLE, YAHYA HIJAZI
AND GABRIEL LEVIN

➔ ←

Ruth Ozeki is a Canadian-American novelist, filmmaker and Soto Zen priest. Her novels include *My Year of Meats* (1998), *All Over Creation* (2003) and *A Tale for the Time Being* (2013), which won the LA Times Book Prize and was shortlisted for the Man Booker Prize. She is currently the Elizabeth Drew Professor of Creative Writing at Smith College.

To A

HAROLD PINTER (1930–2008)

⇁ ↽

ANTONIA FRASER

In the summer of 2007 Harold wrote me a poem. As usual he worked on it not so much secretly as privately before reading it to me . . . I burst into tears and in some ways shall always remain upset by it, as well as deeply, unbearably moved. It was written, as it turned out, about eighteen months before Harold died. But at the time, and ever after, I recognized it for what it was: a farewell. The first line in particular gave me a jolt. Rather touchingly, Harold did not seem particularly upset by my reaction since he was busy being pleased with himself for the concept of the dead missing the living rather than the other way around. He kept exclaiming over it in a contented manner: 'Isn't it an original idea, the dead missing the live?' 'Yes, but . . .'

To A

I shall miss you so much when I'm dead,
The loveliest of smiles,
The softness of your body in our bed.
My everlasting bride,
Remember that when I am dead,
You are forever alive in my heart and my head.

(2007)

→ ←

Antonia Fraser has published numerous historical works, including *Mary, Queen of Scots* (1969), *Cromwell, Our Chief of Men* (1973), *The Gunpowder Plot* (1996) and *Perilous Question: The Drama of the Great Reform Bill* (2013). She has also written nine Jemima Shore crime stories and two volumes of memoirs, *Must You Go? My Life with Harold Pinter* (2010) and *My History: A Memoir of Growing Up* (2015). She was appointed DBE in 2011.

Road Signs

CAROLINE BIRD (1986–)

→ ←

JUDE KELLY

My daughter is a poet and when she was twenty she wrote this piece, 'Road Signs', which she told me is about her and me.

Of course, most children write a story or do a little drawing about their mum and we keep it in the attic forever along with early school photos and handmade Halloween outfits. But a professional child's ruthless appraisal of your contribution to their life is to be feared. If she had written a version of Philip Larkin's 'This Be The Verse', with those piercing lines 'They fuck you up, your mum and dad', I would certainly have cried. But very different tears from those I shed when I read this piece.

We live our life as parents with a constant background noise of anxiety about whether we're finding the right balance between praise and admonishment, structure and freedom, smothering and laissez-faire. And I suspect many of us still often feel as confused as in our adolescence, and for my own part I've never really known what a 'Grown Woman' is. A mature, self-assured, wise and patient person? Is that really me?

But I read Caroline's poem and it told me that I'd done something useful as a mother and as a grown up. It made me cry with relief – and gratitude.

Road Signs
(on the way to my work)

You were travelling a grey motorway.
You had a baby in your lap
with enormous green eyes
and a scarily large head.
You parked the car in a lay-by, sat on the roof,
held her high like a trophy,
joked 'one day all of this will be yours.'

Then you crunched the leaves from the trees
into a mess of green and said 'these are leaves.'
Baby said 'show me something else.'
You showed your baby the ocean
and baby said 'salty.'
You showed your baby mud
and baby covered herself in mud.
You showed your baby a grown man
and baby said 'let's give some green
to that man and some ocean and some mud.'
So you did. Then you showed your baby tears
and baby said 'ocean?'
Then you showed your baby blood
and baby said 'salty,'
and you said 'don't drink that,'
and baby said 'muddy man,'

and baby said 'bloody leaves,'
and baby said 'the ocean is a green man with salty blood'
and you recognized your baby's madness.

Now I am a young woman
I travel the grey motorway alone
and women who are not my mother
teach me grey, acidic truths:
weather-girls trapped in thick glass buildings,
situation comedies with boldly coloured sofas,
mini-markets flourishing in meteorite craters.
I pop the cork on my strange vinegar bottle,
try to become unrecognisable.

But when I return,
the swaddling-wraps still steaming on the floor
from when I evaporated, my mother
pours green-tea, shows me the tyre-marks on her wrist –
souvenirs from the grey motorway.
Then she points at the sky and says
'those are clouds,'
then she takes me outside and says
'this is sunlight'
then she pushes me down a well and says
'that is darkness'
and I mean to say 'obviously,'
but I say 'bandages, griddle and ouch'
I say 'griddle my bandages,'
I say 'sunlight my ouch'

I say 'bandaged clouds griddle darkness with sun'
and I run inside to find a pen
and my mother shouts 'A is for Apple!'
and I write and I write and I write
our sweet green poem.

(2009)

➔ ⬅

Jude Kelly has directed more than 100 theatre and opera productions for, among others, the National Theatre, the Royal Shakespeare Company and English National Opera. Founder-director of the West Yorkshire Playhouse, she is artistic director of London's Southbank Centre.

Small Comfort

KATHA POLLITT (1949–)

→ ←

PATRICIA CLARKSON

This poem raises to the level of dignity the 'small comfort' that means so much to all of us. And it reminds us how soul-shattering it is to be deprived of the everyday joys we often take for granted. In the end, it's these small human touches that sustain us – both as a person and as a people. They make us who we are.

Small Comfort
Coffee and cigarettes in a clean cafe,
forsythia lit like a damp match against
a thundery sky drunk on its own ozone,

the laundry cool and crisp and folded away
again in the lavender closet – too late to find
comfort enough in such small daily moments

of beauty, renewal, calm, too late to imagine
people would rather be happy than suffering
and inflicting suffering. We're near the end,

but O before the end, as the sparrows wing
each night to their secret nests in the elm's green dome
let the last bus bring

love to lover, let the starveling
dog turn the corner and lope suddenly
miraculously, down its own street, home.

(2009)

→ ←

Stage, screen and television actress **Patricia Clarkson** has won two
Emmy awards for her recurring role in *Six Feet Under*, an Academy
Award nomination for *Pieces of April* (2003) and a Tony nomina-
tion for her role as Mrs Kendal in *The Elephant Man*. She has also
appeared in many films, from *The Untouchables* (1987) to *High Art*
(1998), *The Station Agent* (2003), *Cairo Time* (2009) and *Learn-
ing to Drive* (2014).

Home

WARSAN SHIRE (1988–)

→ ←

SUNNY JACOBS

This poem speaks to me on many levels. The pain of isolation. Being a stranger in a land where one should feel embraced. Having no home to return to. Being misunderstood. Losing one's whole world. Being separated from one's family and loved ones and not being able to help them. Becoming collateral damage in an unjust situation. Losing one's humanity. Overwhelmed by circumstances not within one's control. And the saddest part is that we can help them if we choose – we have become inured to the mayhem and negativity that we see and hear on the news daily and nightly. But a picture or a poem, which is a series of pictures in words, can reach our hearts. This poem, 'Home' by Warsan Shire, reached into my heart and brought tears to my eyes. The connection is made.

Home
no one leaves home unless
home is the mouth of a shark
you only run for the border

when you see the whole city running as well

your neighbours running faster than you
breath bloody in their throats
the boy you went to school with
who kissed you dizzy behind the old tin factory
is holding a gun bigger than his body
you only leave home
when home won't let you stay.

no one leaves home unless home chases you
fire under feet
hot blood in your belly
it's not something you ever thought of doing
until the blade burnt threats into
your neck
and even then you carried the anthem under
your breath
only tearing up your passport in an airport toilets
sobbing as each mouthful of paper
made it clear that you wouldn't be going back.

you have to understand,
that no one puts their children in a boat
unless the water is safer than the land
no one burns their palms
under trains
beneath carriages
no one spends days and nights in the stomach of a
        truck
feeding on newspaper unless the miles travelled

means something more than journey.
no one crawls under fences
no one wants to be beaten
pitied

no one chooses refugee camps
or strip searches where your
body is left aching
or prison,
because prison is safer
than a city of fire
and one prison guard
in the night
is better than a truckload
of men who look like your father
no one could take it
no one could stomach it
no one skin would be tough enough

the
go home blacks
refugees
dirty immigrants
asylum seekers
sucking our country dry
niggers with their hands out
they smell strange
savage
messed up their country and now they want
to mess ours up
how do the words

the dirty looks
roll off your backs
maybe because the blow is softer
than a limb torn off

or the words are more tender
than fourteen men between
your legs
or the insults are easier
to swallow
than rubble
than bone
than your child body
in pieces.
i want to go home,
but home is the mouth of a shark
home is the barrel of the gun
and no one would leave home
unless home chased you to the shore
unless home told you
to quicken your legs
leave your clothes behind
crawl through the desert
wade through the oceans
drown
save
be hunger
beg
forget pride
your survival is more important

no one leaves home until home is a sweaty voice in your
    ear
saying –
leave,
run away from me now
i dont know what i've become
but i know that anywhere
is safer than here.

(2009)

→ ←

Since her release in 1992, after being sentenced to death and
spending seventeen years in prison in Florida for a murder she did
not commit, **Sunny Jacobs** has campaigned against the death pen-
alty and for other human rights. Her story was told in the 2005 TV
film *The Exonerated*, in which she was played by Susan Sarandon.

for women who are difficult to love

WARSAN SHIRE (1988–)

→ ←

TAIYE SELASI

I first encountered this poem, and this poet, in 2013, when a dear friend sent me the heartbreaking lines: 'you can't make homes out of human beings / someone should've told you that.' As a lifelong lover of words, a worshipper at the altar of their power, I was familiar with the feeling of finding myself reflected in the musings of a stranger. And still this was different. In exactly eight words a writer – a woman? a man? a poet? a philosopher? I hadn't the foggiest idea – had exposed my deepest hope and my deepest fear to the clear, searing light of day. For a decade at least, I'd been trying to make a home out of a human being for a heart too wild, too fragile, too trusting, too distrustful to be housed. The moment I read these lines of Shire, I knew what I'd been seeking (a home) and knew that my longest, truest search was utterly, utterly doomed. I wept for my foolishness. I wept for my homelessness. I wept for what seemed my incurable loneliness.

Many months passed, perhaps a full year, before I found the poem. As happens in the age of the internet, the disembodied quote was ubiquitous, posted to pages as if it were a standalone admonition. 'You can't make homes out of human beings. Someone should've told you that.' I can still remember the day I chanced upon the entire poem. My heart skipped a beat when, right near the end, I found those few true words. I'll never forget what happened next. I read the end of the poem. 'You are terrifying / strange and beautiful / something not everyone / knows how to love.' The ancient wound that Shire had exposed with eight words she closed with thirteen more. I wept for my strangeness. I wept for my beauty. I wept for the beauty of truth plainly told. Poetry alone can do this: touch, with the fewest of phrases, our raw beating hearts. Warsan Shire, a poet like no other I know, healed mine.

for women who are difficult to love
you are a horse running alone, feral
and he tries to tame you
compares you to an impossible highway
to a burning house
says you are blinding him
that he could never leave you
forget you
want anything but you
you dizzy him, you are unbearable
every woman before or after you
is doused in your name
you fill his mouth
his teeth ache with memory of taste
his body just a long shadow seeking yours
but you are always too intense
frightening in the way you want him
unashamed and sacrificial

he tells you that no man can live up to the one who
lives in your head
and you tried to change, didn't you?
closed your mouth more
tried to be softer
prettier, more quiet
less volatile, less awake
but even when sleeping you could feel
him travelling away from you in his dreams
so what did you want to do love
split his head open?
you can't make homes out of human beings
someone should have already told you that
and if he wants to leave
then let him leave
you are terrifying
strange and beautiful
something not everyone
knows how to love.

(2009)

➔ ←

The writer and film-maker **Taiye Selasi** has published various short stories – including 'The Sex Lives of African Girls' (2011) and 'Aliens of Extraordinary Ability' (2014) – and the novel *Ghana Must Go* (2013). She was executive producer of *Afripedia*, a documentary series about urban African creatives, and has recently completed *Exodus*, a feature documentary about global migration.

Sixty Years After

DEREK WALCOTT (1930–)

→ ←

CHIMAMANDA NGOZI ADICHIE

Walcott is one of the great poets of the English language. This is not as complex as many of his other poems that I love but it is the one poem that I am moved by in a haunting, lingering way. That deeply mortal longing for immortality permeates it. And its plainspoken tone heightens its nostalgia, its beautiful melancholy. It makes me think of all the 'what could have been' situations in my own life, even those yet to happen (because they will, as they do in all human lives) and it makes me mourn them in the lives of others.

We will always imagine other lives we might have led.
We will always grieve what will now never be.

Sixty Years After
In my wheelchair in the Virgin lounge at Vieuxfort,
I saw, sitting in her own wheelchair, her beauty
hunched like a crumpled flower, the one whom I thought
as the fire of my young life would do her duty

to be golden and beautiful and young forever
even as I aged. She was treble-chinned, old, her
   devastating
smile was netted in wrinkles, but I felt the fever
briefly returning as we sat there, crippled, hating
time and the lie of general pleasantries.
Small waves still break against the small stone pier
where a boatman left me in the orange peace
of dusk, a half-century ago, maybe happier
being erect, she like a deer in her shyness, I stalking
an impossible consummation; those who knew us
knew we would never be together, at least, not walking.
Now the silent knives from the intercom went through us.

(2010)

→ ←

The works of Nigerian-born novelist, playwright, short-story writer
and poet **Chimamanda Ngozi Adichie** include the novels *Purple
Hibiscus* (2003), *Half of a Yellow Sun* (2007), which was subse-
quently adapted into a feature film and won the Baileys 'Best of the
Best' Prize in 2015, *Americanah* (2013) and the essay *We Should
All Be Feminists* (2014).

John, this is the sea (from *Something Like the Sea*)

PHILIP GROSS (1952-)

→ ←

DEBORAH BULL

I've always been moved by our inability to navigate the void between ourselves and our fellow men – our frequent failure to find the words or the courage to say whatever it is we really want to say. I remember the first time this struck me. I must have been nine or ten and I was watching Yul Brynner and Deborah Kerr in *The King and I*. It was a scene close to the end, where the obstinate king refuses to admit he wants the governess to stay. I rushed outside to my mother, in floods of tears. 'He couldn't tell her,' was all I could manage, between the sobs. Years later, the lyrics of Mike Rutherford's 'The Living Years' still choke me, too painfully close to those 'stilted conversations . . . between the present and the past' with my mother, towards the end of her life. 'Extraordinary how potent cheap music is,' as Amanda says, in Noel Coward's *Private Lives*.

This poem by Philip Gross is from an anthology called *Deep Field*. The poems explore the gulf that develops between Gross and his father, John, a wartime refugee, as he began, in his nineties, to lose his several languages, first to deafness and then to profound aphasia. Through Gross's adroit use of language, space and silence, we come to understand John's story, the poet's deep connection with his father and, in particular, the love of words they shared. 'Where can you go back to once you've lived in language?'

Deep Field is a tribute not just to the poet's father – 'What am I working on, you used to ask . . . Building your memorial like something grand raised out of rubble, out of the redundant stuff of language . . .' – but to language itself: its power to communicate, mediate, define.

Gross grew up in North Cornwall and, throughout, the recurring image of the sea (and the way it connected father and son) is a metaphor for the fluid, shifting and wordless sounds that become John's verbal landscape. The effect of the poems is cumulative, but I've chosen 'John, this is the sea' from the first of three sequences titled 'Something Like the Sea'. In this poem, I'm caught by the pain of Gross's loss: not only of a common language, but of his father, as the conventional parent-child relationship is inverted through time and the unstoppable progress of his aphasia.

John, this is the sea from *Something Like the Sea*

and don't imagine that I mean it
beautifully, We know

how silt- and salt-thick sea is,
how uneasy, ulterior, insatiably

lightless once the play
of surfaces is done with,

how it nearly did for us
both once, near Polzeath,

in the undertow. Sea:

it's in the dissolution business,
particles suspended for a while

round sunken matter, dis-
cohering, smoking off in strands,

and don't imagine that I want
to go there. But

(you're saying, in the slur
and backwash of your deep aphasia

where we're drowning men clutching at words)
we're there already. Where we were

at the very beginning.

(2011)

→ ←

Once a principal dancer with The Royal Ballet, **Deborah Bull**
went on to become Creative Director of the Royal Opera House.

Also a writer and regular broadcaster, she has been a member of Arts Council England, a Governor of the BBC, and is now Director, Culture at King's College London and a member of the Arts and Humanities Research Council.

The Ballad of True Regret

SEBASTIAN BARKER (1945–2014)

➜ ᐸ

HEATHER GLEN

I heard Sebastian Barker read this poem at his last poetry reading, delivered from his wheelchair in the chapel of Trinity College, Cambridge, at dusk on a winter day in January 2014. Nobody who was there will ever forget that reading. The poet was obviously dying (he was to die two days later), but radiant with enjoyment – of poetry, of the occasion, and of the family and friends assembled there. The chapel was beautiful, lit with candles; the mood was of celebration. But all were aware of the darkness descending outside.

What moves me in this poem is its unashamed expression of the rawness of primitive feeling: the desolation and the loneliness of saying goodbye for ever to the world the living share. Its poignancy lies in its lack of polish, its Blake-like ballad form. It offers no euphemisms, no consolation. In a succession of vivid cameos it simply evokes and celebrates a life intensely loved. This, with naked directness, is the passion of true regret.

The Ballad of True Regret

Never to look on the clouds again,
Never the flowers, nor seas.
Never to look on the sparkling rain,
Nor Easter in the trees.

Never to tread on the forest floor
Mottled with pools of light.
Never to open the kitchen door
To walk in the starry night.

Where will I be, when you are here
So full of life, so full of cheer,
And I am in no place we know
Where I and all the living go?

What of the sound of the distant bells
Announcing a man and wife?
What of the children collecting shells
On the beach at the start of life?

What of Gloucestershire burning blue
As far as the eye can see?
What of the table set for two
With a candle burning free?

Never to look in those smiling eyes
Where my sweetheart is to be found.
Never to look on the morning skies
With the dew of the night on the ground.

What of the lakes where the wild swans glide
And the moorhens dart in the reeds?
What of the woods where the goslings hide
And the rabbits are nibbling seeds?

Never to watch how the wild wind blows,
Nor the rainbow takes to the sky.
Never to see how a daughter grows,
Nor a son, to a parent's eye.

Never the honeyed yoghurt
Spooned by the jocular don.
Never the finished work of art
With the artist looking on.

Gone are the many moments
Like snowflakes into a hand.
Gone are the blissful, intimate scents
Of love in a vanished land.

(2012)

➔ ←

A Professor of English Literature at Cambridge University, and
Fellow of Murray Edwards College, Australian-born **Heather Glen**
has published studies of William Blake, the Brontë sisters and Wil-
liam Wordsworth. She is the editor of *The Cambridge Companion
to the Brontës.*

This Skin That Carry My Worth

EARL MILLS (1952–)

→ ←

AZAR NAFISI

I recently met Earl Mills, an African-American man in his sixties who had been illiterate until the age of forty-eight. Learning to read and write created in him this unimaginable urge to write poems. It is so amazing that writing poetry became his way of re-discovering both the world and himself, the self that until then had remained silenced, ashamed, hidden.

This Skin That Carry My Worth
This skin that carry my worth, May be darker than
You like

We don't all look alike,
We vary from high yellow, to jet black.
Our lips are thick and full, nose flat and wide
The women's hips are nice and round,
And they sway from side to side.

Our tragic past has only made us strong
What was meant to break us, now impales us, like a
    break,
It shows us, the past so that we can gleam, the future.

By standing on the shoulder of men and women of our
    past!
With skin that may be darker than you like.
Their blood that forged through their tragic past.
With hope they gleam today and tomorrow.

So when you look at me.
This skin that may be darker than you like.
Has been to hell and back.
Yet we stand tall with our heads up and shoulders back.

This dark skin that carry my worth,
Was not my choice it was my birth.
This Skin That Carry My Worth.

(2013)

➜ ⬸

A fellow at Johns Hopkins University's School of Advanced International Studies, Iranian-born **Azar Nafisi** is the author of the *New York Times* bestsellers *Reading Lolita in Tehran* (2003), *Things I've Been Silent About* (2009) and *The Republic of Imagination* (2014). She has taught at Oxford University and several universities in Tehran.

An Unseen

CAROL ANN DUFFY (1955-)

→ ←

IMTIAZ DHARKER

In this poem there is a devastating sense of an unrealized future, of things not allowed to be born. It is written in the context of war, but the sense of loss grows outward through the poem to encompass all bereavement and all lost love.

The marvellous thing about this poem is the way it puts language to work so that the loss is told in the grammar.

The punctuation in the first two lines suggests a reluctant departure, the turning and wishing to return, then the confusion of absence, breath snagging on the commas. In the second verse all the sounds become smaller and begin to fade away. The poem is as much about time as about love, 'all future / past, an unseen', leading up to that heartbreaking twist of tense and language, 'Has forever been then? Yes / forever has been.'

I have this poem above my table where I can read it every day. Whenever I come to the last line my breath catches in my throat.

An Unseen

I watched love leave, turn, wave, want not to go,
depart, return;
late spring, a warm slow blue of air, old-new.
Love was here; not; missing, love was there;
each look, first, last.

Down the quiet road, away, away, towards
the dying time,
love went, brave soldier, the song dwindling;
walked to the edge of absence; all moments going,
gone; bells through rain

to fall on the carved names of the lost.
I saw love's child uttered,
unborn, only by rain, then and now, all future
past, an unseen. Has forever been then? Yes,
forever has been.

(2013)

→ ←

Imtiaz Dharker is a poet, artist and documentary film-maker. Awarded the Queen's Gold Medal for Poetry in 2014, her collections include *Purdah* (1989), *Postcards from god* (1997), *I speak for the devil* (2001), *The terrorist at my table* (2006), *Leaving Fingerprints* (2009) and *Over the Moon* (2014). She has also had solo exhibitions of drawings in India, London, New York and Hong Kong, and writes and directs films, many of them for NGOs in India, concerning shelter, education and health for women and children.

City Horse

HENRI COLE (1956–)

→ ←

JOYCE CAROL OATES

'City Horse' will break your heart.

A first reading evokes sympathy, pity, sorrow for the exploited, doomed creature. A second reading evokes sympathy, pity, sorrow, for us all . . .

The 'city horse' is both an individual horse, that has been used, misused, exploited, and discarded – an image of suffering, speechless animal life. At the same time, the 'city horse' is an aspect of ourselves, fated, helpless, used-up and discarded eventually as well – by nature, and by time. We, too, are animals, and yet we are 'citified' – we have been made unnatural by our increasingly mechanized and impersonal society. 'At the end of the road from concept to corpse' – what an unsettling line! Like many of Henri Cole's poems, 'City Horse' suggests a surreal landscape, or a dream landscape, that blossoms into an urgent reality before our eyes.

'City Horse' is one of a number of poems by Henri Cole about creatures not 'human' – among my favourites are 'Hens', 'Shrike', 'Hairy Spider', 'Bats', 'Dolphins' and 'Pig' (all from *Touch*). When I read 'Pig' to my writing class at San Quentin Prison while I was teaching there several years ago, the inmate-writers were riveted by the image of the stalwart if doomed pig; they saw immediately the connection between a pig being taken to the slaughterhouse that has made a futile gesture toward freedom and their own captive lives. The poet's sympathy for all sentient life is beautifully conveyed in the most formally controlled and precise language.

Henri Cole was born, in 1956, in Fukuoka, Japan (where his soldier-father was stationed) and grew up primarily in Virginia. His portrait of himself as a young child suggests an early, precocious air of 'doubleness' – the child who is emotionally involved with his parents, especially his mother, and yet the child who is a perpetual observer, a witness to his own life. This 'doubleness' suffuses Henri Cole's work with its startling juxtapositions, its beautifully precise and musical lines, and its enigmatic images that repay many readings. Often in Henri Cole's poetry there is an air of urgent, intense 'confession' – yet the reader is not altogether certain what is being confessed, or how to interpret the poet's emotional engagement with his material. This mystery of irresolution leads us to read more of Henri Cole, as we are led to reread the enigmatic 'City Horse'.

City Horse
At the end of the road from concept to corpse,
sucked out to sea and washed up again –
with uprooted trees, crumpled cars, and collapsed
    houses –
facedown in dirt, and tied to a telephone pole,
as if trying to raise herself still, though one leg is broken,
to look around at the grotesque unbelievable landscape,
the color around her eyes, nose, and mane (the dapples of
    roan,

a mix of white and red hairs) now powdery gray –
O, wondrous horse; O, delicate horse – dead, dead –
with a bridle still buckled around her cheeks – 'She was
    more smarter than me,
she just wait,' a boy sobs, clutching a hand to his mouth
and stroking the majestic rowing legs,
stiff now, that could not outrun
the heavy, black, frothing water.

(2013)

The American writer **Joyce Carol Oates** has published many award-winning novels, from *With Shuddering Fall* (1964) to *The Man Without A Shadow* (2016). Her other books include plays, novellas, short stories and twenty works of non-fiction as well as ten volumes of poetry. She has taught creative writing at Princeton, New York University, Berkeley and Stanford.

Vigil

JEREMY ROBSON (1939–)

→ ←

MAUREEN LIPMAN

I have read Jeremy Robson's poem at several literary events and the room becomes silently electric. It is both mature and accessible, and has an incessant rhythm of rain on roofs and blood pounding in veins. It is about being aware of the lessons of history as well as the struggle to have compassion. I identify deeply with this poem.

Vigil
I don't accuse,
am on my guard,
that's all.

I won't forget they tried
to wipe my broken
people
from the earth – no,
not them, of course, too

young, their fathers or their
fathers' fathers – not even
them, perhaps.
Be fair.

They might, who knows,
have been among those
righteous brave who
in reaching out their hands
sealed their own fate,
or simply those who turned
away, afraid. Perhaps.
Impossible to conceive
the fear, the shadows of
the night, the bootsteps
on the stair.

Now, a life-time later,
alone beneath the Bahnhoff's
amber lights, incessant
rain machine-gunning the
roof's grim glass, I tell
myself the hordes
I watch there, fighting
their way towards the waiting
trains – *achtung* – late for
work or hurrying home,
that they could not
themselves have heard
the shots, the muzzled
cries, the dogs, the

clank, clank, clank
of the nightmare trucks
departing on cue for their
one-way journey to Hell
(from which of these platforms
I wonder – one, two?)

and that looking back
aghast, perhaps, at those black
Wagnerian scenes, history
to them, however obscene,
that they, contrite perhaps,
would wash their hands
in innocence at night –
not, like some demented Lady
Macbeth, scrub scrub
scrubbing
to expunge the dead, as
those accursed others should.
Sins of the fathers
heavy on their head.
Be fair.

And yet, and yet…
It's seventy years since
that war began, but if
I, a Jew, scion
of that haunted race,
forget, who will remember,
and if none remembers, the
dead are truly dead.

I don't accuse,
am on my guard,
that's all.

(2014)

→ ←

The British actress **Maureen Lipman** has appeared with both the
National Theatre and Royal Shakespeare Company, and in such
West End productions as *Re:Joyce*, *Oklahoma!* and *Daytona*. Her
television credits range from *Coronation Street* and *Doctor Who* to
Agony, *About Face*, *Ladies of Letters*, *Treasures of Britain* and *Bull*.
Radio includes the BBC's *To Hull and Back*. Her films include
Educating Rita (1983) and *The Pianist* (2002).

Sentenced to Life

CLIVE JAMES (1939–)

→ ←

GERMAINE GREER

'Sentenced to Life' was written by Clive James in May 2014. It is a simple, straightforward response to his own approaching death. In eight highly wrought five-line stanzas he summarizes his feelings of guilt and regret, and his new awareness of the preciousness of the small things he had never had time for during his busy working life. I am the person he met after he had walked the mile to the town centre of Cambridge to get his breakfast, who is supposed to have told him that he must be aching for his homeland. The last line is a more correct memory of what was for me an important interchange. The last two stanzas connect across the years with another of Clive's poems that I can't read without crying, 'Go Back to the Opal Sunset'. It is the poet's fate to die in exile, but then exile is, some say, a life-long human condition.

Sentenced to Life
Sentenced to life, I sleep face-up as though
Ice-bound, lest I should cough the night away,

And when I walk the mile to town, I show
The right technique for wading through deep clay.
A sad man, sorrier than he can say.

But surely not so guilty he should die
Each day from knowing that his race is run:
My sin was to be faithless. I would lie
As if I could be true to everyone
At once, and all the damage that was done

Was in the name of love, or so I thought.
I might have met my death believing this,
But no, there was a lesson to be taught.
Now, not just old, but ill, with much amiss,
I see things with a whole new emphasis.

My daughter's garden has a goldfish pool
With six fish, each a little finger long.
I stand and watch them following their rule
Of never touching, never going wrong:
Trajectories as perfect as plain song.

Once, I would not have noticed; nor have known
The name for Japanese anemones,
So pale, so frail. But now I catch the tone
Of leaves. No birds can touch down in the trees
Without my seeing them. I count the bees.

Even my memories are clearly seen:
Whence comes the answer if I'm told I must
Be aching for my homeland. Had I been

Dulled in the brain to match my lungs of dust
There'd be no recollection I could trust.

Yet I, despite my guilt, despite my grief,
Watch the Pacific sunset, heaven sent,
In glowing colours and in sharp relief,
Painting the white clouds when the day is spent,
As if it were my will and testament –

As if my first impressions were my last,
And time had only made them more defined,
Now I am weak. The sky is overcast
Here in the English autumn, but my mind
Basks in the light I never left behind.

(2014)

→ ←

Since Australian-born **Germaine Greer** moved to the UK in the mid-1960s, she has established a reputation as a leading authority on feminist and literary matters. Her many books include *The Female Eunuch* (1970), *Daddy, We Hardly Knew You* (1989), *The Change* (1991), *The Whole Woman* (1999) and *Shakespeare's Wife* (2007).

Afterword by Sebastian Faulks

I cried so much reading this collection that my family thought I was concealing some terrible news. Look at 'Daylight Robbery' by Paul Henry on page 236. I have witnessed exactly the scene he describes with both my sons, but didn't stand back far enough at the time to see the experience for what it was. The poem made me cry with a mixture of happiness and sorrow in reliving what Paul Henry captures so well, but also with regret that I did not sufficiently inhabit the moment in my own life.

As a teenager first enthusiastic for poetry, I was thrilled by the Romantic idea of a 'spontaneous overflow of powerful feelings', taking as its origin 'emotion recollected in tranquillity'. Making the reader cry seemed to me then an important part of what a writer, even in prose, should aim to do. But when you're older and your life has provided more 'powerful feelings' than you really have the stomach for, the poetic appetite may turn to something more austere or contemplative. A notable feature of this collection is to remind one that such a polarity is false; many of the tears that follow are evoked not by rhetoric but by a reflective winnowing.

Is there then a hierarchy of tears, a snobbery of sobs? I suppose we might agree that the tear you shed when the footman in *Downton Abbey* rose to become a village schoolmaster was a cheap one, while the gasp you sighed at the closing lines of 'The Waste Land' was more dearly bought. In which case, where do we place 'Donal Og', with which the book starts? My wife first showed me this poem three years ago and I found it literally unreadable – a wild lament, for sure, but a curse as well. It's like the adagio from Mahler's Fifth or the distant strains of 'Danny Boy': it goes straight to some lachrymal centre with almost no need of 'meaning'. Does that imply that a neural trick is being played – the poetic equivalent of adding umami paste to your workaday stew? I'm not sure. But I do think it's powerful, and in another place may try to work out how it's done – if I can bear to re-read it.

Linguists and neurologists have suggested that poetry speaks to a primitive part of the brain (some have even tried to plant a flag there, somewhere in the right hemisphere). Rhythm and rhyme helped oral bards remember verses before writing was invented; they were mnemonics. But there is something more complicated and interesting in the deep structure of grammar and the brain. Without venturing into the language of neuroscience, it is roughly this: poetry speaks to a vestigial part of the mind that was more active at the time *Homo sapiens* was becoming what she/he is. When we respond to poetry we engage a part of our being that is more primitive and in some way purer than the consciousness available minute by minute to our busy left-side brain.

Yet I have two friends, both cultured, one indeed a novelist, who cannot respond to poetry; they are deaf to it. One night my wife and I read out loud to them first 'Eden Rock' by Charles Causley, then Sean O'Brien's wonderful 'Fantasia on a Theme of James Wright', with tears pouring down our faces; yet they felt nothing beyond a faint embarrassment. Perhaps they are more evolved, more fully *sapiens* than we are, having shed the primitive neural connections to which poetry most directly speaks.

Most emotional effects in poetry are connected with death. The foreground may contain abandonment, love, ageing, fleeting joy; but the background is almost always the darkness of what awaits. Tennyson's 'Ulysses' provokes an unusual kind of tear in this respect: it's more than an old man's rage against the dying of the light; the force of myth and rhetoric are harnessed to evoke a noble indifference to fate, almost a hunger for extinction. The effect is what they call 'stirring', but it's more than that – because the words evoke the universal through the particular and make us improbably complicit in the desires of an 'idle' king, while the comparison of sea waves to land furrows appeals to something ancestral, proto-human, vanished from modern experience.

Few of the verses selected are what we might call love poems, and perhaps this is because successful love poems (as opposed to the playful lust poems of Donne and Marvell, both absent here) are almost impossible to write. A poet may evoke the individual in a description of how he/she is adorable or may appeal to the universal, because we all know what we mean by love; but it's very hard to inhabit the intersection of the two; and that is the place where poetry is usually formed. I think A. L. Kennedy's comments on the 'private' closing of her Elizabeth Barrett Browning sonnet nicely sum up part of the problem. 'When You are Old' by W. B. Yeats comes near, but is it really a poem of love or loss? 'After great pain' by Emily Dickinson takes us cleverly round the back of the subject; Dickinson joins hands with us in compassion for our imagined loss without describing hers. And that is a sophisticated formal coup, made possible by the poem's simple diction.

The range of poetry in this anthology is so wide that it's hard to see patterns or common themes. With which proviso, I imagine few readers will fail to be struck by how stark many of the poems are: here are writers who have not flinched when looking at the *lacrimae rerum*. John Clare in 'I Am' speaks so plainly that it takes a moment to understand the awfulness of what he is saying – that he wishes to be apart from any human being, alone with grass, sky and his creator. The choices of Catherine Mayer, 'Listen!' and its response 'No Solace Here', are more than unflinching; their candour verges on the shocking. I cannot find words for the emotions involved in Susanna Tomalin's beautiful poem or in her mother's sharing of it.

With such poems in mind, it's hardly surprising to record, as well, a lack of sentimentality. There are some dangerous choices; but I think Margaret Drabble's introduction convinces us that 'Say not the struggle naught availeth' is well made and Joan Baez persuades us to look again at Leigh Hunt and find something properly touching in his cautionary verse. And as Carol Ann Duffy and Joanne Harris suggest, there is enough ballad-like artistry to keep Yeats's 'Song of Wandering Aengus' on the right side of whimsy.

It is interesting that three of the greatest poets here – Shakespeare, Jonson and Wordsworth – are represented by their elegies for children, and I feel Pam Ayres is right to claim Wordsworth's prose as poetry; it does the business of poetry as well as the verses of the other two. Interesting, as well, though not perhaps surprising, is the number of First World War poems chosen: widows, mothers and sisters have always borne their share of agony from this largely male-conceived and male-enacted mania.

It may be clear by now how much I have enjoyed this anthology. It has given me fresh pleasure in familiar poems and introduced me to exciting new voices. There is hardly a misfire to be found; and if I may never quite be convinced by the work of Pablo Neruda, I know that to many readers he will be a delight and a gateway to other poets. As for any male/female differences between this and its precursor volume chosen by men, I leave that to the editors, reviewers and readers to debate. What I know for sure is that the art of poetry, as exemplified here, transcends all gender issues, real or disputed.

When I was asked to write this Afterword, I said yes because I love poetry and admire the work of Amnesty International; I had no idea what a superlative collection I would be asked to comment on. And neither, I presume, had the editors when they first drew up their ambitious international list of contributors and set about ways of trying to contact them. They launched a fleet of hopeful messages in bottles on the sea. What has returned to port is a 'ship of gold under a silver mast'.

→ ←

The British novelist **Sebastian Faulks** made his name with his historical 'French trilogy', *The Girl at the Lion d'Or* (1989), *Birdsong* (1993) and *Charlotte Gray* (1998). His other novels include *A Fool's Alphabet* (1992), *Human Traces* (2005), *Engleby* (2007), *A Week in December* (2009) and *Where My Heart Used To Beat* (2015). He has also published authorized sequels to Ian Fleming's James Bond cycle in *Devil May Care* (2008), and P. G. Wodehouse's Jeeves and Wooster series in *Jeeves and the Wedding Bells* (2013).

Why Amnesty thinks this book is important

When Anthony and Ben Holden asked Amnesty to partner on this book's predecessor, *Poems That Make Grown Men Cry*, we were immediately intrigued because the concept probed a well-known and discriminatory gender stereotype: that men shouldn't cry.

This new book, on the other hand, could seem to perpetuate the cliché that women are the ones to cry. But look closer. All the contributors are women who have punched through glass ceilings, overcome enormous odds and in some cases extreme dangers. Yet all of them value poetry and all are willing to take the time to nominate words that move them to tears. And it doesn't take much delving to see what is so interesting: a collection of poems from the eighth century to the present day, each one presented with a personal and stimulating introduction by the woman who chose it. Not surprisingly, some of these women are less willing to admit to tears than others: this is the twenty-first century, after all. Women still have battles to fight.

In some countries those battles are extreme. Afghanistan, for example, which is one of the most dangerous places in the world to be a woman and where, particularly in Taliban-controlled areas, a woman caught writing poetry risks severe punishment. An Afghani woman whom we invited to contribute to this anthology declined, for fear of reprisals against her family. Many women poets have been attacked: Nadia Anjuman was beaten to death when she was only twenty-five. Her killer was her husband, a university academic. Her crime was to have 'shamed the family' by writing poems that are even more poignant in hindsight, including the lines 'Oh, I will love the day when I break out of this cage / Escape this solitary exile and sing wildly'.

Today, with marvellous defiance, many Afghani women have turned to poetry to poke fun at their repressors in a deliberate – if highly risky – act of rebellion. A women's literary society, Mirman Baheer, has grown up whose members write *landai*, traditional Pashtun poems that are short, funny and furious. The poets preserve their safety (and in regions outside Kabul their anonymity) through the collective nature of their writing, and their witty, ribald words are widely shared. Poetry here is at the very heart of women's rights. But they continue to face harassment, threats and attacks from the Taliban or other insurgents, from government authorities, powerful commanders and warlords, and even from their own families. They risk death for the right to be heard.

In *Poems That Make Grown Women Cry*, one of the most famous censored poems is on page 136. Russian Anna Akhmatova did not dare to keep a copy of *Requiem* even as she wrote it for fear of arrest. Instead she whispered it, line by line, to close friends, and when they had committed the words to memory she burned the scraps of paper on which they were written. It wasn't published until after Stalin's death.

Imprisonment didn't deter Ukrainian-born poet Irina Ratushinskaya, who was sentenced to seven years in a Soviet jail in 1983. She was so desperate to write that she scratched verses onto bars of soap with a pin or the burnt end of a matchstick. She memorized her words and then washed them off the soap. She also wrote poems in minute handwriting onto four-centimetre-wide strips of paper, rolled them up in cigar-shaped plastic tubes sealed with a match, and managed to persuade prison staff or soldiers to smuggle them out to her dissident husband Igor Gerashchenko in Moscow. He passed them on to Western journalists. Knowing that Irina needed paper, Igor used to write her abusive letters full of threats of divorce and poisonous insults, all concentrated in a small square in the middle of the page that left plenty of blank paper on the borders. He knew this mail would always be delivered to her.

In liberal societies it's hard to comprehend that poetry could provoke such wrath. But censorship always grows out of fear – presumably of poetry's power to liberate minds and souls. Poetry provides women with opportunities for self-expression and education. Extremist groups fear the empowerment of women and don't want equality, so they crush poetry as a means of denying women's rights.

Simone de Beauvoir said that 'man is defined as a human being and a woman as female'. As with *Poems That Make Grown Men Cry*, most of the poems in this anthology are written by men. This may reflect the even-handedness of the women who have chosen them without allowing questions of gender to determine their choice. However, it will also be a consequence of traditional education systems, as throughout history male poets have been more encouraged and revered than women and have inevitably dominated literature lessons in school. Often it's when we are sitting in classrooms as impressionable teenagers that poetry first speaks to us – poems by men, being more available, had more chance to affect us. The poems that first moved us to tears are often those we return to throughout life, again and again.

Poetry is an age-old creative sharing of human feelings, thoughts and hope. Poems spark inspiration and aspiration – to truth, justice and freedom. We see this clearly in both of these fine anthologies, *Poems That Make Grown Women Cry* and its predecessor for men. One of the leading poets in Afghanistan today, Partaw Naderi, writes of 'a silenced song on my lips'. He knows that if you strike dumb the singer and the song, the poet and the poem, you also dumb the audience. That is what censors seek to achieve – to repress not just writers but the expression of feelings and identity and the evolution of ideas. *Poems That Make Grown Women Cry* shows us how poetry helps us to forge our many ways through life and to become who we truly are.

We at Amnesty are profoundly grateful to all the contributors. Most of all, we thank Anthony and Ben Holden for their generosity in sharing this beautiful project with us.

Nicky Parker
Publisher

Amnesty International UK
The Human Rights Action
   Centre
17–25 New Inn Yard
London EC2A 3EA
www.amnesty.org.uk
sct@amnesty.org.uk

Amnesty International USA
5 Penn Plaza
New York
NY 10001
www.amnestyusa.org

Acknowledgements

Just as this book was going to press, a moving letter arrived from Chelsea Manning, prisoner no. 89289 at the US Disciplinary Barracks at Fort Leavenworth, Kansas, apologizing for her failure to deliver an entry in time for publication.

When first approached, Chelsea had indicated that she was very keen to contribute. That same week in August 2015, however, two years into her thirty-five-year prison sentence for whistleblowing on military abuses, Manning's rights were abruptly curtailed for possession in her cell of such 'prohibited property' as the autobiography of Malala Yousafzai, the US Senate Report on Torture and the issue of *Vanity Fair* featuring a cover story on Caitlyn Jenner, as well as a tube of expired toothpaste. These restrictions coincided with a devastating development in her fight to be treated in accordance with female grooming standards that would allow her to grow out her hair, like other women prisoners. The military again rejected the request, which had come through Chelsea as well as her doctors. Just as she was placed on numerous restrictions, including denial of access to the prison library, where she had planned to research her defence against these charges as well as her entry for this book, she was also dealing with the reality that she would be subject to male grooming regulations including forced hair cuts every two weeks. 'I really appreciated the offer,' she wrote, 'and very much wanted to make a contribution. I am very, very sorry.' So are we, Chelsea, so are we. Your plight is symbolic of so many contributors to this volume, as indeed of many of the poets represented.

Manning's letter reached us via Amnesty International, with whom we again feel privileged to have worked on this project. As with our last anthology, *Poems That Make Grown Men Cry*, we wish to thank our inspirational partners (and now friends) at Amnesty UK, especially Nicky Parker for her invaluable support and Lucy Macnamara for her tireless efforts, alongside their colleagues Maggie Paterson, Kehinde Brown and Bill Shipsey of Art for Amnesty.

We are also profoundly grateful to Ian Chapman and Suzanne Baboneau of Simon & Schuster UK, for commissioning this second volume; they have again proved paragons among publishers. Thanks also to their colleagues Gill Richardson, Elizabeth Preston, Helen Mockridge, Emma Harrow, Rik Ubhi, Dawn Burnett, Sarah Birdsey, Jo Whitford and Charlotte Coulthard. A similar salute goes to Jon Karp of Simon & Schuster US and our editor in New York, Emily Graff.

Heartfelt thanks are due to Jessi Gray for her indefatigable and ingenious work in licensing the rights to all these poems and obtaining releases from contributors, co-ordinating a very complicated delivery process and providing useful general counsel throughout.

We are also indebted, as ever, to our representatives Gill Coleridge and Cara Jones of Rogers, Coleridge & White.

Thanks are due to two kindred spirits: William Sieghart and Susannah Herbert of the Forward Prizes and National Poetry Day, for their generous support of our endeavours amid their own continuing crusade for poetry. The staff at the excellent Saison Poetry Library in London's Southbank Centre have also proved obliging beyond the call of duty.

For help in locating or following up with contributors, or other kind assistance, we are indebted to: Michael Almereyda, Sophie Baker, Morwenna Banks, Cindy Blake, Melvyn Bragg, Lucy Bright, Barbara Bruni, Lucas Calhoun, Duncan Campbell, Tessa Carnegie, John Clare, Mercedes Yolanda Cooper, Naomi Cooper, Rowan Cope, Fred Courtright, Tom Drewett, Ava DuVernay, Mark Eckersley, David Edgar, Harold Evans, Barbara and Ken Follett, Jeremy Gaines, Natalie Galustian, Ann Goldstein, Roy Greenslade, Katie Haines, David Hare, Amrei and John Harrison, Alex Hornby, Damon Lane and Mary Jane Skalski, Jillian Longnecker, Simon Millward, Harriet Mitchell, John David Morley, David Pring-Mill, Clare Reihill, Alan Samson, Elizabeth Sheinkman, Joe Shrapnel and Anna Waterhouse, John Shrapnel, Ben Silverstone, Peter Straus, Rick Stroud, Faye Ward, Jane Wellesley, Debbie Whitaker. Many other friends, agents and/or assistants have also gone to considerable trouble to help us along the way; we apologize for not naming them all here.

Thanks to the eminent novelist Sebastian Faulks, one of the contributors to our original male volume, for generously agreeing to write the Afterword for the female.

We also remain indebted to Richard Cohen for his significant role in the genesis of this dual-anthology project, and to Kathy Robbins.

All Holdens in both our lives have again lent invaluable support and assistance, especially Salome, George, Ione, Sam, Ursula, Rosemary, Joe and Amanda.

Above all, we wish to thank our contributors for so generously giving of their time and energy not merely in sharing a poem that they cannot read without a tear, but also in taking the trouble to explain why. Their short essays are truly remarkable. And it goes without saying that we are very much in the debt of the poets themselves, as we will always remain.

Index of Contributors and Poets

Index of Titles of Poems

Index of First Lines

Credits, Copyrights
and Permissions

'Verses from My Room' by Susanna Tomalin © Susanna Tomalin, 1979. Reprinted with kind permission of Claire Tomalin.

'Sonny's Lettah' from *Selected Poems* by Linton Kwesi Johnson (first published as 'Mi Revalueshanary Fren' in Penguin Classics 2002, Penguin Books 2006). Copyright © Linton Kwesi Johnson 2002, 2006. Reprinted with permission of the author.

'Grow Old With Me' © 1980 Lenono Music. Written by John Lennon. Used by kind permission/All Rights Reserved.

'I shouldn't have started these red wool mittens' from 'Ten Cheremiss (Mari) Songs' from *Notes on the Possibilities and Attractions of Distance: Selected Poems 1965–2000* by Anselm Hollo. Copyright © 1983, 2001 by Anselm Hollo. Reprinted with the permission of The Permissions Company, Inc. on behalf of Coffee House Press, www.coffeehousepress.com.

Introduction by Lydia Davis to 'From Ten Cheremiss (Mari) Songs' by Anselm Hollo, copyright © 2016 by Lydia Davis, all rights reserved.

'The Kaleidoscope' from *New Selected Poems* by Douglas Dunn. Copyright © 2003 by Faber and Faber Ltd. Reprinted with permission of Faber and Faber Ltd.

'On Squaw Peak' from *Human Wishes* by Robert Hass. Copyright © 1991 by Harper Collins.

'Perfection Wasted' from *John Updike: Collected Poems 1953–1993* (Hamish Hamilton 1993) by John Updike. Copyright © John Updike, 1993. Used by permission of Alfred A. Knopf, an imprint of the Knopf Doubleday Publishing Group, a division of Penguin Random House LLC. All rights reserved.

'Clearances, 3 and 5' from *Open Ground: Poems 1966–1996* by Seamus Heaney. Copyright © 1998 by Seamus Heaney. Reprinted with permission of Farrar, Straus and Giroux, LLC and Faber and Faber Ltd.

Introduction by Sarah Waters to 'Clearances, 3' by Seamus

'Point Blank', 'Polish Village', 'Haste' from 'Battalion 101' from *Collected Poems* by Micheal O'Siadhail. Copyright © 2013 by Bloodaxe Books. Reprinted with permission of Bloodaxe Books.

'The Last Part' from *Goodbye* by Deborah Keily. Copyright © 2015 by S Films (MYA) Ltd and Deborah Keily. Used with kind permission of the Keily estate.

'Our Neighbours' from *Island of Dreams* (Noctua Press, 2007) by Felix Dennis, reprinted with kind permission of the Felix Dennis Literary Estate.

'Revenge' by Taha Muhammad Ali, translated by Peter Cole, Yahya Hijazi and Gabriel Levin, translation copyright © 2015 by Peter Cole, Yahya Hijazi and Gabriel Levin. Reprinted with permission of the translators.

'To A' from *Various Voices* by Harold Pinter. Copyright © 2001 by Faber and Faber Ltd. Reprinted with permission of Faber and Faber Ltd.

Excerpt from Various Voices, copyright © 1998 by Harold Pinter. Used by permission of Grove/Atlantic, Inc. Any third party use of this material, outside of this publication, is prohibited.

Introduction by Antonia Fraser to 'To A' from *Must You Go* by Antonia Fraser. Copyright © 2015 by Antonia Fraser. Printed with permission of the author.

'Road Signs' from *Watering Can* by Caroline Bird. Copyright © 2009 by Carcanet Press Ltd. Reprinted with permission of Carcanet Press Ltd.

'Small Comfort' from *The Mind-Body Problem: Poems* by Katha Pollitt. Copyright © 2009 by Katha Pollitt. Reprinted with permission of Melanie Jackson Agency, LLC., and Random House, an imprint and division of Penguin Random House LLC. All rights reserved.

'Home' by Warsan Shire, copyright © 2009. Reprinted with permission of the author and flipped eye publishing limited.